# *Praying from the* Third Dimension

Printed in the United States of America 2016—First Edition

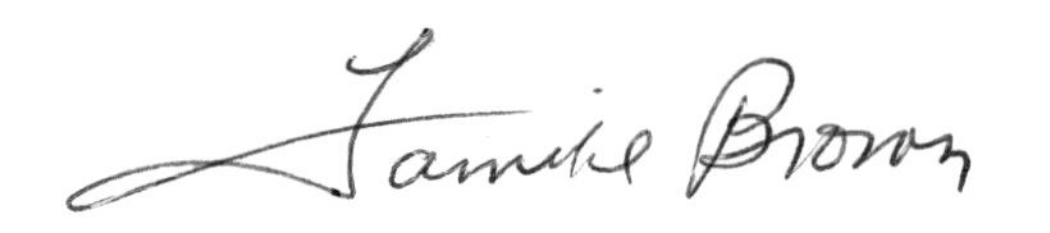

## *Dedication*

*To my parents, Dr. Tom Bynum and Katherine Bynum, for raising me in a house that was constantly filled with prayer and affording me the opportunity to see the results in prayer*

*To Mother Estella Boyd, for your teachings on the importance of living a consecrated life.*

*To Mother Gertrude Stacks, for your revelatory teachings on the depths and the realms of prayer.*

## *Special Thanks*

*To My Pastor, Apostle John H. Boyd Sr; for your constant commitment to encouraging me in 5:00am Prayer.*

*Thank You to all who made the release of Praying from Third Dimension possible.*

*To Earnest Washington and the team for an amazing photoshoot. Special thanks to* ***Assauna (Katie Blue) James*** *– Hair and* ***GMMA*** *– makeup.*

*Special thanks to* ***Design Envy*** *in Garden City, New York for the beautiful and unique jewelry designs used in these photos. I appreciate you!*

*To* ***William Young*** *for Xclusive Designs by Sir Will. Thank you for your countless hours of graphics work. Late nights and early mornings, design changes and fast turnarounds – you never once complained or delayed the vision. Your sacrifice is blessings so many!*

# Contents

# Preface

## MYJOURNEY INPRAYER

My mind reflects back on the beginning of my journey. Even as a child, I always enjoyed observing different levels of the anointing, and watching the Holy Ghost move upon powerful men and women of God. Of the many evangelists that I have seen in my lifetime, one in particular, Missionary Everett, stands out. Whenever our pastor called her to the podium, she would pray, and the anointing hit the room! She was mighty in the Spirit.

Having grown up in the Church of God in Christ, I went to conventions and watched ministers like Mother Elsee Shaw, a great intercessor of our time and Sister Kelly, an awesome intercessor who still ministers in prayer to this day; and of course, my grandmother, Doretha Bynum was one that I watched very closely and intently. Her prayer ministry boasted of the power and presence of God.

I remember standing in amazement as spiritual transitions would take place in these services, watching how an auditorium or building would be transformed into a sanctuary— people standing, praying, with a prayer

leader on the microphone—and then suddenly, the whole atmosphere would shift. I could literally feel a "weight" descending upon the people.

It would "sit" in the building, getting thicker and thicker, and then shift, turn again…and the room would fall into silence.

Slowly, the sounds of groaning and wailing, and the cries of those who were travailing in tears would begin to rise up to heaven. Then suddenly, heaven's door opened and God stepped down into the midst of His people. I would look around, amazed, at people's faces that confirmed their hearts and minds had embraced the Lord's answer. This was—and still is—an awesome sight.

People go to concerts, or to hear somebody preach, sing, or play an instrument—and these things can be incredible—but nothing compares to watching prayer in process. Prayer brings a right now result, entering into our Father's presence and experiencing all that He is.

History has seen many gifted ministers of God, but no one has ever mastered prayer.

Some have mastered playing an instrument; others have mastered the art of preaching—but no one can claim "mastery" over prayer. God is the only Master of it. He owns the eternal rights to prayer, and that is why it does not matter how many people have written books on this topic. God has and always will unfold something new.

Prayer is ongoing communion with God to the point that we begin to know His heart and mind. Can anyone fully, and completely, experience all that God is?

The process of prayer never ends, because God is eternal. He is the first, and the last, the Alpha and the Omega. This is why I believe Luke 18:1 says, "…men ought always to pray, and not to faint." God has commanded us to pray without ceasing, because there will always be something that we need to learn about Him.

## GOD CALLED ME TO THE NEXT LEVEL

As the years passed, and my mother attended conventions, I would always say, "Whatever you do, bring me back some prayer tapes." And she did. Listening to prayer cassettes became my favorite pastime. I would love hearing people like C.H. Mason, Mother Shaw, or Etheo Clemens pray. Then I came across Larry Lea's Could You Not Tarry One Hour?, and once again, God transformed my ability to enter His presence.

God called me to the ministry of prayer in 1998. (I remember it well, because that was the year that I preached a message called "Refiner's Fire" at a conference hosted by Bishop T.D. Jakes.) I had fallen asleep downstairs on the couch in my den. At about 4:30 a.m., the sound of something hitting the floor jarred me to consciousness. Since I had been attacked many times by demonic forces that had entered a room (or had spiritual warfare in the middle of the night), I immediately sat up and began speaking in tongues, because I felt like this was yet another spiritual warfare.

I looked around, and then noticed a plaque that had fallen to the floor from the mantle. It had been a gift from a friend. It was a special gift to me because it spelled and described my name. I got up, put the plaque back in its place, and went back to sleep. Bam! It hit the floor again. When I got up this time, I said to myself, "Okay, I know that I set this plaque back up correctly; for it to keep falling off of the mantle, something is up." Upset, I started binding the enemy; because I felt that he was trying to mess with my name (the description on the plaque was so powerful).

Once again, I put the plaque back on the mantle, and went to sleep. A third time, it fell. When I woke up, I heard the Lord say, "I am calling you to prayer." Then He said, "Look at the clock." It was 5:00 a.m.

God told me, "If you do not pray, this is what the enemy desires to do to the power of the name that I am establishing for you in the earth. He desires for you to hit the ground." Then He said, "Prayer, for you, is not going to be optional. It is mandatory. It is your lifestyle. You will not be able to survive the spiritual warfare that is coming against you, because of your assignment, if you do not pray."

That day, I started praying at 5:00 a.m. In fact, many mornings I did not even need an alarm—and I am not a morning person! Nevertheless, my eyes would automatically open at 5:00 a.m., like clockwork. Bam! I was awake, and I started having personal experiences with the Lord.

Much of what people see happening in my life right now was birthed out of intercession in 1998.

People may look at me and say, "The favor of God is on her life," or "The hand of God is with her," but the reality is that God revealed things to me in prayer, and I had to birth them out. I birthed out the nation. There were times that I was on my basement floor for hours, starting at 5:00 a.m.—not realizing how long I had been there! God would show me masses of people, and I would travail in prayer for hours. God was saying, "You are called to the nation long before you get to the nation. You are called to them long before you get to them. The reason they will be able to receive you is because you have already met in the Spirit realm."

Yes, I believe that the people I preach to now are those whom I have already called forth in the Spirit realm. God placed them in my loins. They were my "assignment" years before I stood before them in the natural!

No, I do not believe that I am drawing a random crowd. People do not just hear about the name, Juanita Bynum, and come to hear me minister. God has already designated these people in the Spirit realm; they are part of my spiritual assignment.

When you begin to realize the power of prayer, how it governs and channels your future, then you will truly understand why you should pray.

Though Peter wavered, he was able to stand again because Jesus had said, "But I have prayed especially for you [Peter], that your [own] faith may not fail..." Lk. 22:32, (AMP) Though Peter stumbled, he could not ultimately fail—because prayer had already gone up before him. The Holy Spirit said that Peter had not "watched and prayed" with Jesus in the Garden of Gethsemane, so he fell when his faith was tested. Yet ultimately, Jesus restored Him, because Peter's victory had already birthed out in prayer.

Prayer reaches into the future, stabilizes us, and sealsour destination.

Prayer puts us in the position where Satan cannot cancel our destiny, because that prayer has already been answered! Things that you pray for now, that God will do in the future, cannot be altered...they have already been answered and sealed in the Holy Ghost!

Jesus had to agonize in prayer in the Garden of Gethsemane, because He already knew His spiritual assignment, but He had to break through the fleshly realm that did not want to submit to the assignment. The Bible says that He was "slain from the foundation of the world" Rev. 13:8, so Jesus was not slain on the cross! That is where the process was completed, where the manifestation took place from what had already been declared in heaven.

If Jesus agonized in prayer so that His flesh would not get in the way of the Spirit, then we need to pray just like He did. We must pray so the flesh realm does not hinder what God has already proclaimed that we are supposed to be, and have, in the Spirit realm.

When we agonize in prayer, our Spirit man leaps beyond the flesh realm! Always remember that everything you are going to be and do is connected to what you are praying right now. You do not get to the future, and then pray!

Through my experiences in prayer, I have come to understand one thing. Everything that exists was first created in the Spirit realm, and then it is manifested in the flesh. The things that are happening in Christendom now in the flesh (worldly) realm, already existed in the Spirit realm.

When I realized that prayer was the key to my future, I began to spend every morning in prayer.

The Lord also instructed me at that time to keep

a prayer journal, so I began to write down the things that He would tell me. Every morning, I would pray and write down what God said.

Amazingly, I can read back through my prayer journals and see how God has brought these things to pass.

It is a blessing when people say, "I have been praying for you," but there is nothing like seeing a manifestation of the glory of God that results from your own prayers! I had been praying since I became a Christian, here and there, until that morning in 1998. I was what you would call an Outer Court pray-er (we will get more into this later, as we study the three levels of prayer).

God was calling me to the third dimension of prayer, which means I started to spend unlimited time with Him. I have heard people say, "If you start out by praying 7 minutes a day, that will be okay; then move to 15 minutes a day, etc." When God called me to the third dimension of prayer, I prayed for hours! God gave me a time of day to pray when I did not have to rush my time with Him, because He wanted to begin to do things for me and through me. Supernaturally.

When I accepted this call, I began to see results. Things started to change in my life at a speed that was so rapid, it almost scared me. There were times I almost began to believe that I was going to die, but God was trying to help me understand that this is where He wanted me to live. He said, "The blessings that are now coming upon your life at this accelerated rate is how I desire for all of My people to live."

If He took me to the next level in prayer, He will do the same for you.

## GOD BEGAN TO REVEAL HIS PATTERN

Over the last 3 years, the Lord began to deal with me about going "behind the veil." This new pattern steadily gained a significant, and unusual, influence in my heart and mind. After I had completed volume I of Morning Glory, I thought that the following year, we would release the next music CD, Morning Glory, volume II. This is when an unusual process began, and I did not see the pattern until later.

When we operate in the Spirit realm, we simply do what we are "led" to do, or have been arrested by the Lord to do—without taking time to examine the pattern of the Lord, how He works, and makes things happen. God does everything according to a pattern. He operates according to divine order. Many times, we do not pay attention to this when we are "flowing" in the Spirit.

As we learn to pay close attention to what God is doing, then we will see beyond the natural realm. In other words, something we may "naturally" have thought was an isolated incident is actually the beginning of something in the Spirit. Something that looks like it is just starting to happen could very well be coming to an end, while something else is in the middle stages of spiritual development. What you see and experience reflects where you are in God's pattern.

What am I trying to say? God's pattern, from the beginning, has been revealed through the Tabernacle of Moses. He gave specific instructions then, and He has continued to deal with the body of Christ according to the three stages of this pattern: The Outer Court, the Holy Place, and the Most Holy Place.

God's pattern of prayer also deals with our character, and as a result, our walk with Him. It never changes. For example, think about how our churches are built. There is usually an outer foyer that leads to the inner sanctuary. From there, you go to the altar. In every sanctuary, the altar leads us into the presence of God. In the Tabernacle, God's manifest presence remained in the Most Holy Place, between the cherubim on the Ark. This "altar" is something that we have not been able to recreate, because it requires us to constantly repent and seek the Lord. We must prepare a place for His presence to "sit" in our earthly tabernacles. As I began to understand the pattern of the Lord, I realized why we are not effective in prayer. We do not move to the next level by living in obedience to God. He has already told us that we are to move from "faith to faith" and "glory to glory." Rom. 1:77, & 2 Cor. 3:18 This means we have to apply faith in God, through prayer, to get to the next level of glory. We are "transformed" as we obey Him.

The first Morning Glory CD was called "Peace." It was powerful, and though we experienced a little bit of warfare here and there, it was not "unbearable." So, the next year, when the Lord told me that we were going to do volume II, I rushed to do it the same way. God had moved to another level, He impressed in my heart that I was to be still, so we released the small cassette, Be Still. I obeyed God, but I did not see the pattern. I did not realize God was doing something that would be "fitly joined together" with what He is doing in my life right now.

The next CD, Behind the Veil, went to another level. Initially, I thought God would give us songs that pertained to His divine presence and that would be that. One thing led to another, and it took us 3 years to complete a project that we thought would be finished in one. Every time we received a song from the Lord, we would enter a new level of warfare.

In January 2000, we received the title cut, "Come Go with Me Behind The Veil," and my Pastor suffered a major stroke. The left side of his body was paralyzed, and we did not know where our church was headed. This thrust us into another level of prayer, which opened my eyes to the pattern of the Lord. God began to show me the 3 levels of prayer, according to the pattern of the Tabernacle: "Outer Court" prayer, "Holy Place" intercession, and abiding in the glory of God "behind the veil" in the Most Holy Place.

I had no idea that I would eventually write about it.

As I pressed past my usual personal prayer time, and the perception that I had "gotten in the loop" in developing my own method of prayer, I knew there was more. Even though I had been getting up every day to pray at 5:00 a.m., and was having awesome experiences with God, His presence was not "resting" on me continually. This is where I feel that you may be right now. You have had some awesome times in prayer, but other days you have felt like you cannot find your way into the presence of the Lord. When this happens, you decided to "just wait" on His presence—but really, you have wondered, "Where has it gone? Where is that awesome experience that I had a few days ago?"

God has revealed to me that His awesome, divine presence can and should be something we experience every time we pray. It was never meant to happen randomly, or moment-to-moment.

Our greatest experience with the Lord in prayer comes when, knowingly or not, we have followed the pattern.

Many times, you do not recognize what you did in order to reach that new level in prayer. You just know on that day, it was different. You started out one

way, turned and went another direction, and

then the "weighty" presence of God came and "sat" in your midst. Suddenly, you were in a supernatural realm with God, one that you had never experienced. You were able to embrace all that He had for you—there were no problems—only answers. Then the next day, you try, but cannot repeat the pattern. It happens over and over again.

God wants us to understand that there is a pattern, a way into His presence. He is calling us to press beyond having an "awesome experience." He wants us to take the time to observe and understand how He works in prayer.

If we understand His pattern, answered prayer can be an everyday reality.

God wants us to know—beyond the shadow of a doubt— that we have touched His throne every time we pray. He wants us to be assured that He hears our prayers, and will answer us.

Prayer becomes a chore when you do not understand the process. When you are "all thumbs" in the presence of the Lord, He may be calling you to another level. God does not want you to be unaware of the enemy's "devices." 2 Cor. 2:11 These devices do not have to be evil attacks that come against you. They can come when you do not recognize and submit to the pattern that will bring you into God's presence. Thus, you can become deceived by the enemy. Realize this—

Satan is offended because we have accepted Christ, but he is not overwhelmed in this offense…because he knows that we will not go deeper in the Spirit without learning the pattern of prayer.

Prayer is the key to our lifestyle, and it is the key to discovering new levels in God. Therefore, we cannot fail to pray. Prayer is the answer to every situation we will ever encounter. Prayer not only changes things, it changes everything, from the end to the beginning. Matthew 9:37– 38 says,

**"Then He said to His disciples, The harvest is indeed plentiful, but the laborers are few. So pray to the Lord of the harvest to force out and thrust laborers into His harvest."**
**(AMP)**

Jesus did not say to thrust laborers into the vineyard; He said that laborers would be thrust into the harvest through people who pray! It has already happened! For example, when you plant and water seeds in a garden, and till the ground, you can wait expectantly for a harvest. So Jesus does not thrust praying people into the tilling process, He thrusts people that pray into a harvest!

When you pray, you come into the manifestation of what already exists! You are thrust into the end result…the finished process!

Remember that everything with God is already "finished," so when you pray, you are not trying to find out how God is going to do His work, you are entering into His finished work. Many times, you do not know that His work is completed because you are too far from Him. Your communication with Him is hindered, because you have not moved from level-to-level in obedience to His Word.

Everything that you need, everything you desire, as we begin this journey back to prayer, has already been "accomplished." You only need to go to the Spirit realm to find the completed harvest, and by way of your physical being, bring that harvest back to the earthly realm. You have to press through the Outer Court into the Holy Place, and then beyond, to the Most Holy Place—where the presence of God lives eternally. You are the chariot that brings the end result of God back into the earth realm.

If someone were to call me and say, "I have a million dollars for you," and they live on the west side of town, and I live on the east side of town, the only thing between me getting the money is transportation. It is the same with the things of God. You have to believe what He says and God uses your mouth, body, and spirit man to transport everything He is and does back to the natural realm.

At every level that you obey, God grants a deeper level of grace and revelation. When you follow God to the third dimension of prayer, you become His means of transportation to receive what He has already "completed" for you, your family, your church, and every area of your life.

So, why not go back to prayer?

# *Introduction*

## OUR JOURNEY TOGETHER

In going back to prayer, we are starting a journey that will ultimately take us to the Most Holy Place. In terms of this series, I am presenting each level of prayer in a separate volume. In this first volume, I talk about the Outer Court, or the introduction to prayer and intercession. Volume II goes into the Holy Place and the last volume will take us into the Most Holy Place, or the Holy of Holies.

How quickly you apply these truths to your life will determine how long your journey will be. In order for you to enter intercession on the third dimensional level, you will need to "do" what you read in each book every single day. God has required this of me, and He will require the same of anyone whom He has called to intercession.

You will notice that I have used Moses' Tabernacle as our model for the life of prayer. I have not attempted to cover every detail of this Tabernacle, because it contains many significant types and shadows. Instead, I am focusing on the areas that God has dealt with me about intercession, both from the scriptures and during my times in prayer with Him. I am sharing with you from my life, and how God has brought me into His Most Holy Place through prayer, intercession, and sanctification.

Each chapter has a "Selah" section at the end, with questions for you to answer, followed by blank journal pages for you to begin your journey in prayer. Yes, God will speak to you! John 10:27 says that you are His sheep, and that you can hear His voice. I want you to take time in each chapter, study the scriptures, prayerfully answer every question, and seek God to hear what He has to say. Write your answers on the journal pages; as well as what He reveals to you in prayer. This marks the beginning of your journey. I encourage you to buy a journal and write everything down that God speaks to you.

As you move from personal prayer in this volume, into intercession (in the volumes that follow), you will begin to hear God's voice more clearly. When God begins to use you to intercede for others, you must be able to hear His instructions about how to pray, as well as how He expects you to live in His presence. You must walk the path of prayer on a personal level before God can use you to effectively intercede for others.

At the end of the final book, there will be a powerful index of Prayer Topics from Pastor Matthew Ashimolowo's The Power of Positive Prayer Bible. You will be able to use it during your prayer times, or anytime that you need to know what the Word says concerning a situation. Over-and-above this, you need to make sure that you are studying the Bible on your own each day, because without it, you cannot be shaped into the image of God. If you do not look like your Father, how can you do His work?

Now I understand, more than ever, why James 5:16 says, "...The earnest (heartfelt, continued) prayer of a righteous man makes tremendous power available [dynamic in its working]." (AMP) Psalm 34:15–20 adds,

**"The eyes of the Lord are toward the [uncompromisingly] righteous and His ears are open to their cry. The face of the Lord is against those who do evil, to cut off the remembrance of them from the earth. When the righteous cry for help, the Lord hears, and delivers then out of all their distress and troubles. The Lord is close to those who are of a broken heart and saves such as are crushed with sorrow for sin and are humbly and thoroughly penitent. Many evils confront the [consistently] righteous, but the Lord delivers him out of them all.
He keeps all his bones; not one of them is broken."**
**(AMP)**

Do you want God to hear your prayers? Keep reading. The truth is going to set you free!

Remember that these books are, first and foremost, teaching tools—so if I repeat something that I have said before, in order to move to the next point—bear with me. I want to make sure that you understand exactly what the Holy Ghost is saying, and see the pattern that He is establishing.

I believe that God is speaking a word for this season and hour. We must hear the Word, and do what it says, or we will not move to the next level.

## THE TRUTH ABOUT THE LORD'S PRAYER

As I became obedient to the Lord in fasting, He began to show me how the Lord's Prayer is actually an introduction to prayer for the immature Christian. It is a starting place. Some believers have been stuck praying this pattern for years! It is supposed to lead us to another level in God; we are not supposed to stay there.

Just like the Outer Court in Moses' Tabernacle, we must "move through" this prayer on our journey to a deeper relationship with God, and deeper revelation. Remember, when Jesus gave this model prayer, He was talking to people that had not heard the voice of God for over 400 years—so He told them something to get them started. They were at the beginning of their journey. They were supposed to grow from there.

If you are called of God to become an intercessor, then the Lord's Prayer is simply an outline, a table of contents. It points to things that you must look into more deeply. It shows a path that you must follow to reach the conclusion of God. What was God's conclusion to me about intercessory prayer? As I sought Him, He said, "If you are going to become an intercessor, then you must go back and look at the pattern of how to become an intercessor," which led me beyond the Lord's Prayer to the Tabernacle.

## ARE WE PRAYING ACCORDING TO GOD'S PATTERN?

It is important that we pray, but it is vital that we pray correctly. Are we experiencing effective prayer, according to God's pattern? If God set a pattern, then He expects us to pray "decently and in order" 1 Cor. 14:40, in harmony with His plan. This is how He wants everything done in His Church!

If we fall out of the pattern for prayer, we can easily begin to pray according to our emotions, which are fruitless, or according to our logical mind, which leads to a spirit of control and witchcraft. You can pray and get an emotional release, or you can pray to ease your mind, but are you praying according to God's pattern? Praying according to God's will has nothing to do with what you think, or how you feel. James 3:17 says,

**"But the wisdom from above is first of all pure (undefiled); then it is peace-loving, courteous (considerate, gentle). [It is willing to] yield to reason, full of compassion and good fruits; it is wholehearted and straightforward, impartial and unfeigned (free from doubts, wavering, and insincerity). And the harvest of righteousness (of conformity to God's will in thought and deed) is [the fruit of the seed] sown in peace by those who work for and make peace [in themselves and in others, that peace which means concord, agreement, and harmony between individuals, with undisturbedness, in a peaceful mind free from fears and agitating passions and moral conflicts]."**
**(AMP)**

If you are living according to God's Word, and praying according to His pattern, God will begin to lead you out of personal prayer and into the deeper realm of intercession. He will lead you to pray according to what is in His heart, not yours. You will begin to pray from a heavenly perspective, not according to earthly wisdom.

On the other hand, if you are not living for God or praying according to His pattern, you will be praying one thing, and thinking another. You will be confessing one thing, and feeling something totally different. There will be constant conflict inside of you. Therefore, You will not be set free, and neither will anybody else. After God had called me to pray at my church (I now lead Tuesday morning prayer), He began, slowly and surely, to reveal the problems we face while we pray. He showed me that when we do not understand the pattern of prayer, we cannot consistently attack a certain realm and gain ground. We cannot consistently come into His presence to receive direction. As Paul said, we end up "beating the air" with our fists, [1 Cor. 9:26, (AMP)] We end up praying with no vision, or direction, and will soon perish. [Prov.29:18]

I have been in church almost all of my life, so I know that if God revealed this to me, you are probably experiencing the same problem; and I promise, if you are truly seeking God in prayer, the revelation He has given in this book will change your life. I know that my prayer life will never be the same, and I prophesy to you that as you embrace this word of the Lord, your prayer life will be "transported" to the next level.

I have prayed that this book would be put into the hands of people in prisons, or in hospitals. I have also prayed that it would fall into the hands of those who do not know the Lord, or how to pray. If this is you, keep reading. Keep turning the pages, and you will meet God. Not only this, you will come to know Him intimately, and hear His voice in your spirit. My friend, God has made sure that you picked up this book, so that He can set you free!

If on the other hand, you are a mature Christian, or maybe you are a Jewish follower of the Messiah, keep reading. God has led me to our spiritual roots. He has unfolded the mysteries of His Word to me as it concerns prayer and intercession. Keep reading. Let us take this journey together.

# Chapter One

## THE GATE: INTRODUCTION TO PRAYER

When you go to a tailor, he takes measurements and then cuts out a pattern to fit your body. If he cuts it the wrong way, according to the wrong measurements, you will not be able to wear the outfit. It will not fit. Though the outfit may be beautiful, it will be useless.

It is the same with God's presence. If we do not structure our prayer life according to the pattern that He has "cut," then He will not be able to step in to our prayers! He cannot commune with us. God cannot step into your time of prayer, unless it has been structured according to the pattern that He has established. Why? Like I said before, He is the master of prayer. God is the only one that knows the measurements of His Spirit. [Rom.8:27]

So, the first step in your journey to third dimensional prayer is to look for the pattern by which we are to enter the presence of the Lord. You must know that answered prayer is not luck, nor does it happen by chance. Look back at the times that you have prayed and received an answer. Most likely, you will discover that you actually prayed according to God's pattern, so you got God's results.

There are times when God sovereignly seems to answer an "out of pattern" prayer. If He does, then God is God! He can choose to act after the counsel of His own will. In other words, as He said to Moses,

***"...I will proclaim My name, THE LORD, before you; for I will be gracious to whom I will be gracious, and will show mercy and loving-kindness on whom I will show mercy and loving-kindness."***
*Exodus 33:19, (AMP)*

Who are we to question God? We must simply learn to come into His presence,

**"Let the wicked forsake his way and the unrighteous man his thoughts; and let him return to the Lord, and He will have love, pity, and mercy for him,and to our God, for He will multiply to him His abundant pardon. For My thoughts are not your thoughts, neither are your ways My ways, says the Lord. Foras the heavens are higher than the earth, so are**

**My ways higher than your ways and My thoughts thanyour thoughts. For as the rain and snow come downfrom the heavens, and return not there again, but watereth earth and make it bring forth and sprout, that it may give seed to the sower and bread to the eater, soshall My word be that goes forth out of My mouth: itshall not return to Me void [without producing anyeffect, useless], but it shall accomplish that which Iplease and purpose, and it shall prosper in the thingfor which I sent it."**
**Isaiah 55:7–11, (AMP)**

There are times when you are not looking for a pattern, times when you do not know what you are actually doing during your time of prayer and you will either enter into communion with God, or you will not. Sometimes you get results, and other times, you do not. Then the frustration begins, and it's not long before you stop praying altogether. This is a tool of the enemy. He wants to discourage you from pressing into God, and hinder God's purpose for your life.

In this last hour, God is bringing us into a new confidence in prayer. This means we are coming into an assurance of who He is, and what He wants; because if we pray according to His pattern, we will get results—every time.

We will see His purpose being accomplished in the earth.

## RETURNING TO THE BEGINNING

As mentioned before, Jesus gave us the Lord's Prayer to begin our journey into the presence of God. It is our divine table of contents. Let us look more closely at Matthew 6:9–13,

> **"After this manner, therefore, pray ye: Our Father which art in heaven, Hallowed be thy name. Thy kingdom come. Thy will be done in earth, as it is in heaven. Give us this day our daily bread. And forgive us our debts, as we forgive our debtors. And lead us not into temptation, but deliver us from evil: For thine is the kingdom, and the power, and the glory, forever. Amen."**

It is through this prayer that we can begin to see the difference between a person who prays, and one who is called to be an intercessor. Many people who are still in the "praying" mode (personal prayer) never make it past the "Give me…" stage with God. On the other hand, intercessors learn to enter His presence asking, "Lord, what do You desire?" The "outline" proves this to be true—it shows all of the ingredients that must be present to become an intercessor.

The Lord's Prayer opens with worship and acknowledging Who God is, the King of the universe. He is Jehovah-Tsidkenu, our righteousness; Jehovah- M'Kaddesh, our sanctification; Jehovah-Shalom, our peace; Jehovah-Shammah, ever present with us; Jehovah- Rophe, our healer; Jehovah-Jireh, our faithful provider; Jehovah-Nissi, our banner; and finally, He is Jehovah-Rohi, our loving shepherd. If you are called to be an intercessor, you should know the Father's names, so that you can call upon Him for every need in the lives of others.

Then the prayer moves into acknowledging the kingdom of God—that which is behind the veil in the third realm that sits on the Ark of the Covenant—along with a request for that portion of God to come toward man. "Thy kingdom come. Thy will be done in earth, as it is in heaven…" signifies our flesh dying on the altar of God.

Then it moves to, "Give us this day our daily bread…" Jesus is the Bread of Life, the

Shewbread, which is always fresh in the Holy Place, sustaining us with the power of the Word. When it says, "And lead us not into temptation, but deliver us from evil," this speaks of maintenance, being held back from evil traps, and sheltered from the attacks of the enemy.

Actually, the door that leads into the Holy Place separates those who enter from anything that tries to follow them in from the Outer Court.

When the verse says, "For thine is the kingdom, and the power, and the glory, forever," it is affirming the eternal, weighty, glory of God that waits behind the veil in the third realm of prayer.

Now that we have a table of contents, it is time to examine every section of God's pattern so that you can discover where you are in your prayer life. Unless you understand where you are in prayer—if you are praying "out of order," or have become stagnated at a certain level of prayer—then you will never know whether or not you are completing the call of an intercessor.

## Unfolding The Pattern of the Lord

We have now arrived at the second step, studying the pattern. As mentioned before, God took me to the Tabernacle of Moses (see the diagram on the title page). In the overall structure of the Tabernacle, there is an entry Gate on the east; the Outer Court where you find the Brazen Laver and the Brazen Altar; the Holy Place, where you come through the Door to find the Golden Candlestick, the Table of Shewbread and the Altar of Incense; and then you move into The Most Holy Place where you pass through the veil to the ark of God.

In each section, the elements have great significance in prayer. These are things that many of us may have looked at and studied for years thinking, "This is just the Tabernacle of Moses, something God gave to him for that time in the wilderness." Not so. The Tabernacle is a divine key into the Divine Presence.

## THE GATE TO THE OUTER COURT

God established the Tabernacle to be a dwelling place for His presence and glory. As part of the plan, He told Moses to build a wall of white linen around the entire Tabernacle

structure to enclose the Outer Court. On the east side of this white linen boundary was the entry Gate.

After Moses set up Israel's camp, the people were situated according to their twelve tribes around the Tabernacle. Regardless of their tribe's location, everyone had to enter through the same Gate. There were no special privileges "... because I am a preacher," or "...because I am a Bishop," or because of some title. Nobody could slip in under the curtain. Ephesians 2:11– 18 says,

**"Wherefore remember, that ye being in time past Gentiles in the flesh, who are called Uncircumcision by that which is called the Circumcision in theflesh and made by hands; that at that time ye werewithout Christ, being aliens from the commonwealth ofIsrael, and strangers from the covenants of promise,having no hope, and without God in the world. But nowin Christ Jesus ye who sometimes were far off are made nigh by the blood of Christ. For he is our peace, who hath made both one, and hath broken down the middle wall of partition between us; (my God),having abolished in his flesh the enmity, even the law of commandments, contained in ordinances; for to make in himself of twain one new man, so making peace; and that he might reconcile both unto God in one body by the cross, having slain the enmity thereby: and came and preached peace to you which wereafar off, and to them that were nigh. For through him we both have access by one Spirit unto the Father."**

When the Israelites approached the Tabernacle, by way of these white curtains, it symbolized coming into the righteousness of God. In prayer, this means that you should begin to examine yourself in light of that pure, white curtain. By looking at this linen, you come to realize that your life does not compare to the purity of that wall that surrounds the Tabernacle. As you walk around the wall of righteousness, beholding what you are not (outside of the His righteousness), you eventually arrive at the Gate to the Outer Court (of personal prayer).

**"For we all have become like one who is unclean [ceremonially, like a leper], and all our righteousness (our best deeds of rightness and justice) is like filthy rags or a polluted garment; we all fade like a leaf, and our iniquities, like the wind, take us away [far from God's favor, hurrying us toward destruction]."**
**Isaiah 64:6, (AMP)**

The Gate could be clearly seen as the Israelites drew near to the east entrance. It was multicolored, according to Exodus 27:16, "And for the gate of the court shall be an hanging of 20 cubits of blue, and purple, and scarlet, and fine twined linen, wrought with needlework: and their pillows shall be four, and their sockets four." These colors actually represent the work of Christ, something we should keep in clear view as we approach God in prayer. Jesus said in John 14:6,

**"...I am the way, the truth, and the life: no man cometh unto the Father, but by Me."**

John said, "In him was life; and the life was the light of men." Jn. 1:4 So Jesus is the life that becomes the light within us— and within the Most Holy Place.

Since Jesus is "the way" to the Father, then the Gate is symbolic of "the way." It is the entrance into the things of God. If you do not understand what these colors represent, right here, you can get off track in your approach to God. If you miss it here, you may never reach the Father. Jesus said in John 10:7–11,

**"...I assure you, most solemnly I tell you, that I Myself am the Door for the sheep. All others who came [as such] before Me are thieves and robbers, but the [true] sheep did not listen to and obey them. I am the Door; anyone who enters in through Me will be saved (will live). He will come in and he will go out [freely], and will find pasture. The thief comes only in order to steal and kill and destroy. I came that they may have and enjoy life, and have it in abundance (to the full, till it overflows). I am the Good Shepherd.**

**The Good Shepherd risks and lays down His [own] life for the sheep."**
**(AMP)**

You have to come to God the Father by acknowledging the works of the Son. I have found it to be very interesting (after God called me to intercession and I began to lead Tuesday prayer at my church), how we approach the throne of God. We have been deceived! We think that

we can come to God any way that we want, and that He automatically hears us.

God said to me, "Do you know how common the church has become when they think they are talking to Me?" You cannot become "common" with God, or you will end up talking to yourself. There are too many stages between the Gate and the Most Holy Place for you to think you can talk to Him like a common man. I have heard people say, "Well, honey, I told God…" Wait a minute! You cannot talk to God like that! You had better back up and repent…fast.

Out of ignorance, we have taken away the reverence of approaching God. We treat

Him like man, and God should be reverenced, lifted...approached with care.

We must learn to come to God by worshipping at the beautiful Gate. The white, fine twined linen represents the righteousness of Jesus Christ as portrayed through the gospel of Luke. It tells about what Christ went through to become righteousness for us. Blue represents Christ as "the heavenly one," according to the book of John. He was with God from the beginning and was the Word made flesh, so that all who believed in Him would be saved. Purple represents the royalty and kingship of Christ, as reflected in the book of Matthew—

He came from a royal lineage to fulfill God's promise to His people. Finally, the scarlet represents Jesus' ultimate sacrifice on the cross, according to the gospel of Mark.

When you enter into prayer through the Gate, you are acknowledging the 4 works of Jesus Christ as expressed in the gospels. You cannot approach God correctly unless you go through His works! If you come to God any other way, you are ignoring the works of His Son, Jesus Christ. You are totally disregarding the fact that He came to earth, was crucified on the cross of sacrifice, rose from the dead, and is now the King of Kings and the Lord of Lords. How can you ignore this? How can you ignore the fact that He is making intercession for you right now, according to Romans 8:34?

Let me break it down further. Jesus stands between the things of God in the court, and all that is in the world. As "the Gate," He is standing there in His first act of intercession for us (and there is intercession at every entry of the Tabernacle). He says, "You are not saved, and you do not know Me as your personal Savior. All that is behind Me within these courts are treasures of My will that you can have, so I am going to stand in this Gate and wait until you get here. I am going to be your way in."

To pass through the Gate, you must accept His works as part of your life. So, you enter into the things of

God by demonstrating your thankfulness for what He has done. Psalm 100:4–5 says,

**"Enter into His gates with thanksgiving, and into his courts with praise: be thankful unto him, and bless his name. For the Lord is good; his mercy is everlasting; and his truth endureth to all generations."**

So many people have not yet heard His voice, yet we as believers take it for granted. Many have not heard Him say, "Come to Me…" Matt. 11:8, (AMP) By being thankful, you acknowledge that you have not come to God of your own accord. If you have come to God, it is because He chose you. In His mercy, He called you into eternity.

Entering the Gate "with thanksgiving" is being thankful according to Psalm 65:4, "Blessed (happy, fortunate, to be envied) is the man whom You choose and cause to come near, that he may dwell in Your courts! We shall be satisfied with the goodness of Your house, Your holy temple." (AMP)

## YOU MUST BE SAVED

If you are not saved, you cannot be thankful for what Christ has done. You can only enter through the Gate by accepting Jesus Christ as your personal Savior—and by receiving His works—or you cannot even get in the front yard, let alone behind the veil! That would be out of the question.

Why would God send His Son to make "the way," and then let you sneak past Jesus into the Most Holy Place?

If you are going to talk to God, you have to come through Jesus' works that are represented in the Gate. In other words, you have to be saved. If you want to come to God, without making any commitment to Him and requesting His help, you are in deception. God is not hearing your prayer!

This can be a tough pill to swallow, but you have to understand. God is a Father, and if He is anything like natural fathers (that we see on the earth), He is not going to take care of a baby that does not belong to Him! A woman comes to a man saying, "I know this is your baby! In December, I was not with anybody but you…" "Prove it!" he says. She had better have more to go on than just what the baby looks like, because if they do a blood test, his daddy is going to show up in the DNA!

So many people in the church are walking around, praying in tongues, looking saved, but what does the Blood test say? Have you been washed in the Blood? God will look at you and say, "You are not Mine, go find your father, which is the devil! I am not obligated to provide you with food to eat, clothes to wear, a job, a sound mind, or peace and joy in your soul. I am not your Father!"

*You must enter prayer by first accepting Christ and then thanking God for "the way."*

I have heard people say that God hears a sinner's prayer, and I agree. Yet according to the Word of God, He only hears a sinner's prayer to repent and be saved. Again, you cannot come to the throne of God as a sinner, interceding for somebody else, and ignoring the work of the Son. It cannot happen, it breaks the pattern of God! Yes, Hebrews 4:16 says, "Let us therefore come boldly unto the throne of grace…", but verse 14 says, "Seeing then that we have a great high priest…let us hold fast our profession."

You can boldly approach God's throne, but by way of the pattern—not by any way you want to come. You must come by way of the pattern of the finished, perfect work of Jesus Christ. When Jesus said, "I am the way, the truth, and the life," He was marking the path to effective prayer. The Gate is "the way," the Holy Place is "the truth," and "the life" shines eternally through God's perfected light in the Most Holy Place.

Gates, doors, and veils are very important in the context of this entire mini-book series, because the same colors are represented in all of them—at every level—representing the finished work of Christ leading us to deeper level with God in prayer.

## THE PERFECT HIGH PRIEST

Let us take a look at why it was necessary for Jesus to become "the Gate." Why did God have to predetermine the works of Christ, and choose these colors? The priests in the Old Testament had been chosen and qualified by God, according to the law that had been given to Israel, and they kept themselves consecrated according to this law. Read with me beginning in Hebrews 7:11,

**"Now if perfection (a perfect fellowship between God and the worshipper) had been attainable by the Levitical priesthood—perfect [look at that word, not worship, not prayer, not praise, but perfect worship, perfect prayer, perfect praise], if this was attainable by the Levitical priesthood—for under it the people were given the Law—why was it further necessary that there should arise another and different kind of Priest, one after the order of Melchizedek, rather than one appointed after the order and rank of Aaron?"**
**(AMP)**

In Aaron's priestly order, the priests would

physically die. That was the only way the order of the priesthood could be changed. So rather than altering priests, and waiting for priests to die—constantly bringing His people under a new priesthood—God in

His own counsel, decided that He would send His Son to become the final, and ultimate, High Priest…the perfect sacrifice.

**"For when there is a change in the priesthood, there is of necessity an alteration of the law [concerning the priesthood] as well. For the One of Whom these things are said belonged [not to the priestly line but] to another tribe, no member of which has officiated at the altar."**
**Vs. 12–13, (AMP)**

Jesus did not need to "officiate" the service of the altar (like an earthly priest), by bringing wood, etc. He climbed up on the altar and became the sacrifice—not the person that officiated—He went into the fire, a pure, willing, perfect sacrifice.

**"For it is obvious that our Lord sprang from the tribe of Judah, and Moses mentioned nothing about priests in connection with that tribe. And this**

**becomes more plainly evident when another Priest arises Who bears the likeness of Melchizedek, who has been constituted a Priest, not on the basis of a bodily legal requirement [an externally imposed command concerning His physical ancestry], but on the basis of the power of an endless and indestructible Life."**
**Vs. 14–16, (AMP)**

This means that Jesus' priesthood did not come from the order of man, but from the third realm. It came from the eternal light, from our eternal Father. Verse 16 continues, "Who has been constituted a Priest, not on the basis of a

bodily legal requirement [an externally imposed command

concerning His physical ancestry], but on the basis of the power of an endless and indestructible Life. For it is witnessed of Him, You [meaning Jesus] are a Priest forever after the order (with the rank) of Melchizedek."

Jesus came "after the order of Melchizedek," because there was no history of Melchizedek's ancestors. There was no record of his beginnings, and no record of his end. He just walked off. It is the same with Jesus. You cannot track a human trail back to God.

Since Jesus came as the Son of God, and there is no end to God, you cannot trace His ancestral end because God is eternal. You cannot project into the future with Christ, because God is not limited to time. He is eternal. No one knows Jesus' end, because He has no end, and no one can understand His beginning, because He was with the Father before the foundations of the world.

Hebrews 7:18 continues, "So a previous physical regulation and command is cancelled…" This means that Jesus was "legally" supposed to come through the rank of Aaron. God broke that tradition, according to His eternal purpose. In kind, Jesus Christ came, broke tradition, reconciled us to God, and introduced us to the Spirit of God. He broke the traditions that were established through the order of Aaron, and took on the lineage of the tribe of

Judah, which means "praise." Let me continue into verse 19,

**"So a previous physical regulation and command is cancelled because of its weakness and ineffectiveness, and uselessness—for the Law never made anything perfect—but instead a better hope**

**is introduced through which we [now] come close to God."**
**(AMP)**

The whole purpose of canceling the old order was to give us an opportunity to draw near to God; not to sit in church, repeat the Lord's Prayer, and think that we have arrived! Jesus came to bring us closer to God—a living, breathing, and vital relationship. Verses 20–23 continue,

**"And it was not without the taking of an oath [that Christ was made Priest], for those who formerly became priests received their office without its being confirmed by the taking of an oath by God, but this One was designated and addressed and saluted with an oath, The Lord has sworn and will not regret it or change His mind, You are a Priest forever according to the order of Melchizedek. In keeping with [the oath's greatest strength and force], Jesus has become the Guarantee of a better (stronger) agreement [a more excellent and more advantageous covenant]. [Again, the former successive line of priests] have made up of many, because they were each prevented by death from continuing [perpetually in office] ..."**

**(AMP)**

The priests rendered a service that was so vital to God's forgiveness of man that He could not afford for it to be hindered or stopped because a priest died; so He chose

an everlasting priest. This is what makes intercession possible. This is what brings us into the Most Holy Place. Since we have a High Priest that forever makes intercession for us, His prayers never stop! He will not be replaced by another priest, so His service and intercession continues throughout eternity.

Hebrews 7:24–25 says, "But He holds His priesthood unchangeably, because He lives on forever. Therefore, He is able also to save to the uttermost (completely, perfectly, finally, and for all time and eternity) …"

When you enter the Gate and pass through those colors, giving thanks to God, you are thanking Him for providing a Perfect Priest. You are looking at the works of Christ, understanding that He is able to save to the uttermost "(completely, perfectly, finally, and for all time and eternity), those who come to God through Him, since He is always living to make petition to God and intercede with Him and intervene for them."

**"[Here is] the High Priest [at the Gate!], [perfectly adapted] to our needs, as was fitting—holy, blameless, unstained by sin, separated from sinners, and exalted higher than the heavens. He has no day by day necessity, as [do each of these other] high priests, to offer sacrifice first of all for his own [personal] sins and then for those of the people, because He [met all the requirements] once and for all when He brought Himself [as a sacrifice] which He offered up."**
**Vs. 26–27, (AMP)**

Jesus does not have to make atonement for His own sins, and this is why He is able to make us more like Him. As His reflection, our lives will come to a different standard, because in the Gate—before you ask God, "Will you... can you?" Someone is already there, representing the power that you are about to receive and walk deeper into the Spirit realm with…this is amazing! You get a glimpse of what will be yours in the third realm of prayer, as you press through the Holy Place of consecration to the third dimension of glory!

Now do you see why you must not only identify with the 4 works (colors) of Christ (in the Gate), but receive and accept them into your own life? To enter prayer, even this first stage, you must begin with Christ…the Perfect High Priest.

## THE POWER OF THE GATE

Many times, we do not understand that the Gate, the Outer Court, the Door, the Holy Place, the Veil, and the Most Holy Place, all work together in prayer. So if you neglect this first Gate, you have neglected an act of God, which can negate a prayer that God is supposed to pre-answer before you ask. Let me make this clear. The Bible says that God knows what we need even "before ye ask." Matt. 6:8 In other words, before you asked Him into your

heart, He was already wooing and drawing you to the Gate, or "the way." So your need for salvation was provided before you asked Jesus to save your soul.

Acts 12, starting with verse 1, helps us to understand the power of prayer and "the Gate."

**"About that time Herod the king stretched forth his hands to afflict and oppress and torment some who belonged to the church (assembly). And he killed James the brother of John with the sword; and when he saw that it was pleasing to the Jews, he proceeded further and arrested Peter also. This was during the days of Unleavened Bread [the Passover week]. And when he had seized [Peter], he put him in prison and delivered him to four squads of soldiers of four each to guard him, purposing after the Passover to bring him forth to the people. So Peter was kept in prison, but fervent prayer…"**
**(AMP)**

Remember, the fervent, effectual prayer of the righteous man avails much! [Jas. 5:16] It gets the job done, not sleepy prayer. Verse 5 says that fervent prayer "was persistently made to God by the church (assembly). The very night before Herod was about to bring him forth, Peter was sleeping between two soldiers, fastened with two chains, and sentries before the door were guarding the prison." Look at the state Peter was in. Does this sound familiar?

I do not care what state you are in, how many chains, how much bondage, how many guards, how much oppression, how much depression… Let me tell you what happened to these Gates!

"The very night…" verse 6 continues, "And suddenly, an angel of the Lord appeared *[Why did an angel of the Lord suddenly appear? Fervent prayer was being made… persistently],* [standing beside him], and a light shone in the place where he was…" vs. 7

Angels "descend" and "ascend" around the Throne of God in the third realm! When angels come to earth, they bring "the light" with them! They bring results from the third dimension down to earth. Let us return to verse 7,

**"And suddenly an angel of the Lord appeared [standing beside him], and a light shone in the place where he was. And the angel gently smote Peter on the side and awakened him, saying, Get up quickly!
And the chains fell off his hands."**

When it is time for you to come out of bondage, God is only waiting for you to get up! Why? Prayer has already been offered up to Him on your behalf. Verses 8–9 continue, "And the angel said to him, Tighten your belt and bind on your sandals. And he did so. And he said to him, Wrap your outer garment around you and follow me. And [Peter] went out [alone] following him, and he was not conscious that what was apparently being done by the angel was real, but thought he was seeing a vision." (AMP)

This is the kind of stuff that God plans to do for us in prayer; spontaneous, miraculous things! When we get God's prayer pattern right, we are going to pray and then think we are seeing a vision, or are dreaming, when the answer comes.

**"When they had passed through the first guard,and the second, they came to the iron gate, which leads into the city. Of its own accord [the Gate] swung open, and they went out and passed on though one street; and at once the angel left him. Then Peter came to Himself and said, Now I really know and am sure that the Lord has sent His angel and delivered me from the hand of Herod and from all that the Jewish people were expecting [to do to me]. When he, at a glance, became aware of this [comprehending all the elements of the case], he went to the house of Mary the mother of John, whose surname was Mark, where a large number were assembled together and were praying."**
**Vs. 10–12, (AMP)**

When Jesus said, "I am the way…" and the way is the Gate—then every other gate must come under subjection to THE GATE. There is a way out, because the way has already been made at the cross.

If you are trying to enter into a job, a business, or if you need passageway into a city, a company, or perhaps a loan from a bank…the Gate… “the way”, is already there! When you come through this Gate, all other gates must open of their own accord—and this is before you even get to the third realm of intercession! This is just the Gate. There is power in the Gate.

So you must understand that when you take that first step, to come by way of Jesus Christ, when you pass through this Gate, then everything you need is already available to you. You only have to finish the pattern to get the end result.

So if I am entering the righteousness of God from the world, I must come by way of Jesus and His works. If I want to go deeper in the Tabernacle and enter the Holy Place, I must go through the Door of Jesus and His works. If I am to enter the Most Holy Place, I have to approach through the veil the same way, by the work of the Son of God.

If we are to travel through 3 dimensions

of prayer to operate where God wants us to be in the Spirit realm, there have to be 3 doors. For every level in prayer, every level in God, you travel the same path—the Way leads to the Truth, which takes you into the Light (in the life of Christ).

After passing through the first entry, the Gate, we demonstrate our thankfulness by doing His works. Jesus said, "I assure you, most solemnly tell you, if anyone steadfastly believes in Me, he will himself be able to do the things that I do; and he will do even greater things than these, because I go to the Father." Jn. 14:12, (AMP)

In the realm of the Outer Court, doing what Jesus did involves pressing deeper into the things of God…to the Brazen Laver, and then to the Brazen Altar of sacrifice. If you really believe in Jesus and have received all that He did, this is your next step in the Outer Court, getting clean and giving up your will.

**The Gate Introduction to Prayer Ex.27:16**

SELAH

# Chapter Two

## THE OUTER COURT: THE EARLY STAGES OF PRAYER

God is constantly moving; He is always in transition. So when you get into the Outer Court, though it is the place that He wants you to begin in prayer, He demands that you do not remain there. You have entered His courts through the Gate of Jesus Christ, but He wants you to go deeper. The perfect example is when the children of Israel left Egypt. They started their journey by way of the wilderness, which was actually a place of blessing until they stayed there too long. This "blessed" place soon became the place of curses.

This leads us to the third step, following God's pattern of prayer.

In order to pass through Outer Court praying, you have to go through every stage that leads to the other side. Many of us enter into the courts of the Lord and embrace "religion," so we never going deeper into His presence. The Outer Court was established when God set the initial boundaries for the Tabernacle in Exodus 27:9–15 & 17–18. This corresponds to the initial conversion experience. Anybody and everybody that asks Jesus to come into their hearts can come into the Outer Court. It is a place of washing and repentance—a place we enter with thanksgiving for what He has done.

The Outer Court was also a place that was lit by the natural sunlight. So though you are being offered eternal light through the plan of salvation, at this point, you are not given eternal revelation. You are still in natural light. If you remain in the Outer Court, though you are saved, you will constantly be exposed to natural elements— fleshly opinions, earthly circumstances— everything that goes on in the natural. You will stay in a place where you are constantly forced to accept the ways and conversations of mortal men.

In Israel, everybody gathered in the Outer Court. Conversations went on about what everybody thought about God, and what they thought about everything else, but if you want to go deeper in the things of the Spirit, you have to keep pressing through. Remember, when the Israelites murmured—complained to each other, talked amongst each other about what God was doing—they got delayed. It stopped their progress. Judgment came. Don't let Outer Court chatter hinder your prayers!

You have to remember that you are on a journey to the Most Holy Place, via the Holy Place, where only a priest can enter. Everybody could come into the Outer Court, but not the Holy Place, and certainly not the Holy of Holies.

When you remain an Outer Court person that prays, nothing about you is consistent. For example, Outer Court people pray "whenever." They pray in emergencies; when something terrible happens and it looks like they are going to be devastated, they cry out to God. Outer Court pray-ers stay in a "praise mode." They admire God, but they never come into relationship with Him. So they never receive the revelation of His heart, and what God desires to do in the earth.

Outer Court pray-ers never get to the stage, "Thy kingdom come…" because they are saying, "I am saved, I know God, I honor God." They never pass through the courts into intercession, because they do not know God well enough to agonize in prayer on His behalf. Outer Court pray-ers are focused on washing, cleansing, and material things. They are always saying, "Give me…I need…"

Remember, you have just come through the Gate acknowledging Who God is—He is our Provider, He is our Peace, He is our Righteousness, He is our Banner of Protection, and so on.

When you stay in the mode of admiring, worshipping, and hallowing the name of God, you are always praying from the position of what you need— "Give me this, give me that"—which keeps you focused on material things.

Outer Court people do not pick up a prayer burden for others, because they are still in their own infant state of being cleansed. They are not sure of where they are in God, so they spend most of their time praying for themselves. In order for the body of Christ to pass through this stage and become intercessors, which means becoming God's ambassador, we have to move deeper into the court to the Brazen Laver, and then beyond that to the Brazen Altar. This is where we begin to submit our own lives to the Word of God, and let go of everything that is not His will. Yes, this is part of becoming an intercessor—and we will talk more about each area later.

## YOU ARE NOT OF THIS WORLD

When the United States sends an Ambassador to some remote, impoverished part of Africa, something "peculiar" happens. When people see him riding down the street, he is in a Mercedes Benz. In that remote part of Africa, he is living in one of the most beautiful houses that you have ever seen. Why?

He lives in that part of Africa, but he is not a citizen of that country. The Ambassador and his family are citizens of the United States, which means our country is obligated to give them the kind of lifestyle they would have if they were in the United States—and not just for their comfort, but for others to look at their lifestyle and see a picture of America. What do people see when they look at your lifestyle? Are you a true ambassador for Christ?

God has already prepared great things for those who love Him, and seek after Him with all of their hearts. We must move through the Outer Court to become His ambassadors! We must obtain the things of God that others lack, because they live in the inferior, earthly realm. We are citizens of heaven, so our lifestyle—the way we carry ourselves, the way we live—must exemplify our heavenly citizenship. We cannot get caught up in the Outer Court.

When you have been born again, you are not a citizen of this world. As God's ambassador, you are to take help from heaven and distribute it to those who live in a place that is "remote" from His kingdom. This is true intercession, standing in the gap for someone else. If you are not doing this, you are praying, but you are not interceding. So many believers get saved and stay in the Outer Court. They never become ambassadors…taking the things of God, standing in the gap of intercession, and passing His blessings on to people that need to receive Him.

## YOU CANNOT STAY IN NATURAL LIGHT

The Outer Court is the first step into the presence of God. It is a wonderful place to be! Yet it only stays wonderful when you are passing through. In the Outer Court, you must get beyond bloops, bleeps, and blunders in prayer. You must also get beyond messing up over and over again in the same, old areas. You have got to move on to maturity, through going to the Brazen Laver and the Brazen Altar, in order to enter the Holy Place.

Like I said before, when you stay in the Outer Court, you live under the influence of the natural light. If you do not press through this stage, you will continue to pray only what you see in the natural. You will not be able to pray by divine revelation, because you have not yet entered the Holy Place, or passed through to the Most Holy Place, where divine revelation lives. You have not yet found the divine presence of the Lord! You are still in the "praise section" of God, along with everybody else who just met Him. Therefore, you pray what you see, and you pray by the example of others, so you do not stretch your faith to know God on a deeper level.

In this stage of prayer, you see the crippled, the sick, the depressed, and those who are without peace, so you pray for healing, deliverance, and peace. Then you look around and nothing has changed. No one has been delivered. No one is walking in divine peace. What is the problem? You cannot remain in the Outer Court! You must pass through to maturity by surrendering yourself to the Word of God, and to His perfect will—then His power begins to fuel your prayers! Hebrews 6:1 says,

**"Therefore let us go on and get past the elementary stage in the teachings and doctrine of Christ (the Messiah), advancing steadily toward the completeness and perfection that belong to spiritual maturity. Let us not again be laying the foundation of repentance and abandonment of dead works (dead formalism) and of the faith [by which you turned] to God..."**
**(AMP)**

It is awful to walk into the Outer Court, acknowledging all that God is and all He is able to do, and then selfishly neglect to offer this same opportunity to others, those who do not know God the way that we know Him. God's purpose (through this pattern of prayer) is to bring you into an awareness of who He is, so that you can stand in the gap for someone else. This is why you cannot remain in the Outer Court!

You cannot continue to pray Outer Court prayers, or make excuses why you do not pray, because every believer has been saved and born again to pray.

Prayer is our ultimate purpose. We were saved so that our prayers could affect the world, because the Word of God has told us, "...The fervent, effectual prayers of a righteous man availeth much." Jas.5:16

Let us look more deeply at this. James 5:16 actually confirms the pattern of prayer, "Confess to one another therefore your faults (your slips, your false steps, your offenses, your sins) and pray [also] for one another, that you may be healed and restored [to a spiritual tone of mind and heart] …" (AMP) Do you see the revelation? Confessing to "one another…" reflects the Outer Court experience. The washing. The cleansing.

It goes on to say, "…and pray [also] for one another…" That means after you undergo the washing and cleansing process, you can make intercession for somebody else, "…that you may be healed and restored [to a spiritual tone of mind and heart] …" Then it concludes by saying, "…The earnest (heartfelt, continued) prayer of a righteous man…"

After you have confessed, after you have repented, and after you have walked in righteousness!

Then it says when you pray for someone, "the earnest (heartfelt, continued) prayer of a righteous man makes a tremendous power available [dynamic in its working] …" Welcome to real intercession.

In that nugget from the book of James, God is saying once again, there is a pattern: The Outer Court person that washes, the person in the Holy Place that maintains, which keeps the Temple in order, keeps the Word of God alive, keeps the Golden Candlestick lit, and so on (we will get into this in volume II). But the consecrated believer who enters the Most Holy Place, where tremendous power is made available—dynamic in its working—in the third realm of intercession.

James 5:17 illustrates a person who knows h o w to tap into the third realm, the place of divine revelation, intervention, strength, and power. "Elijah was a human being with the nature such as we have [with feelings, affections, and a constitution like ours] …" In other words, Elijah was human, just like you and me. God is not a respecter of persons. Anybody that is willing to go beyond the Outer Court can go beyond human limitations.

You might have said to yourself, "I have been saved from sin, but it still looks so glamorous to me…I just keep slipping back into it." As long as you keep slipping back and forth, back and forth, you can never move on to maturity. You will never become an "effectual intercessor." The Bible says that Elijah was a human being with a nature like ours: feelings, affections, and an overall constitution like our own, "…and he prayed earnestly for it not to rain, and no rain fell on the earth for 3 years and 6 months." What power!

A natural man was able to control the weather, because he prayed consistently.

The 18th verse continues, "and [then] he prayed again and the heaven supplied rain and the land produced its crops [as usual]." (AMP)

God makes this same level of power available to anyone that prays "effectually." I am not talking about evangelists, or other people that have "titles." Anybody that is willing to pass through the Outer Court, go through the Holy Place, and into the Most Holy

Place—to the perfected state that is made available to us by God on the mercy seat—is going to get their prayers answered. This praying person, even you, can alter the course of nature. This person can change lives!

## A GLIMPSE OF GLORY

Are you wondering why, since we are studying the Outer Court, I keep mentioning the Most Holy Place? Exodus 25:1–9 says,

**"And the Lord said to Moses, speak to the Israelites, that they take for Me an offering. From every man who gives it willingly and ungrudgingly with his heart you shall take My offering. This is the offering you shall receive from them: gold, silver, bronze, blue, purple, and scarlet [stuff] and fine twined linen and goats' hair, rams' skins tanned red, goatskins, dolphin or porpoise skins, acacia wood, oil for the light, spices for anointing oil and for sweet incense, onyx stones, and stones for setting in the ephod and in the breastplate. Let them make Me a sanctuary, that I may dwell among them. And you shall make it according to all that I show you, the pattern of the Tabernacle or dwelling, and the pattern of all the furniture of it."**

God constructs everything by way of a pattern.

**"They shall make an ark of acacia wood: two and a half cubits long, a cubit and a half wide, and a cubit and a half high. You shall overlay the ark with pure gold, inside and out, and make a gold crown, a rim or border, around its top. You shall cast four gold rings and attach them to the four lower corners of it, two rings on either side. You shall make poles of acacia wood and overlay them with gold, and put the poles through the rings on the ark's side, by which to carry it. The poles shall remain in the rings of the ark; they shall not be**

**removed from it [that the ark be not touched]. And you shall put inside the ark the Testimony [the Ten Commandments] which I will give you. And you shall make a mercy seat (a covering)**

**of pure gold, [now this is the point that I want to get to] ...two cubits and a half long and a cubit and a half wide. And you shall make two cherubim (winged angelic figures) of [solid] hammered gold on the two**

**ends of the mercy seat. Make one cherub on each end, making the cherubim of one piece with the mercy seat, on the two ends of it. And the cherubim shall spread out their wings above, covering the mercy seat with their wings, facing each other and looking down toward the mercy seat. You shall put the mercy seat on the top of the ark and in the ark you shall put the Testimony [the Ten**

**Commandments] that I will give you. There I will meet with you and, from above the mercy seat, from between the two cherubim that are upon the ark of the Testimony, I will speak intimately with you of all which I will give you in commandment to the Israelites."**
**Vs. 10–22, (AMP)**

This is the point, I believe, God is making concerning the pattern of prayer: though we pass through the Outer Court

(cleansing) in this book, and the Holy Place (maintenance) in the next book, God did not declare that He would "meet with us" in either of these places! He did not declare that He would speak on the "cleansing" and "maintenance" levels of prayer. He did not say that He would give us divine instructions, speak intimately about His Word, or discuss His plans for our lives in the first and second realms.

In the third realm, between the cherubim on the mercy seat inside of the Most Holy Place, God declared, **"There I will meet with you..."**
**Exodus 25:22, (AMP)**

You can experience a "presence" of God, simply because you are in the courts of the

Lord. For example, you come to prayer because you have a problem, but you are not committed to God— yet you feel His presence, and you think that you are blessed. Actually, you are feeling the residue of His glory that is coming from the Most Holy Place.

On top of this, the priest would go into the Holy Place and start offering up a "most holy perfume" to God on the Altar of Incense. It would start smelling good, and the scent went all through the Tabernacle. That is why people in the Outer Court, even today, smell the incense of the Lord, thinking that they are blessed, when they are just smelling the residue. Come out of the scent of God, and get into His presence for yourself!

If you want God to speak intimately with you, and if you want to receive divine revelation and divine impartation from Him, you have to go to the third dimension. You have to press through the Altar of Incense to the Most Holy Place—beyond the sweet aroma, and into His glory. You have to hear the revelation of God, from between the two cherubim on the mercy seat, for yourself.

Though you are in the Outer Court, there is a deeper level of prayer that God is calling you to embrace. (In the next book, we will study the furniture in the Holy Place, but we still will not have reached the third dimension!) You must pass through every level, and go to every piece of furniture in the Tabernacle in order to enter the third realm of intercession. This is the level of intimacy with God, where anybody (who has been qualified by Him) can enter and change the course of this world. This is the place where God will change the direction of people's lives through your intercession.

Otherwise, you will constantly knock, hammer away in prayer, and never receive divine information or direction. Your decision to reject the pattern will have closed the door.

You must decide to leave the elementary things, and go on to the deeper things of God.

## THINK OF THAT

**The Outer Court The Early Stages of Prayer Ex. 27:9–15**

*1. Have you been consistent in approaching God through the Gate of Jesus Christ (and His 4 works), and entering His courts with thankfulness and praise? What has changed in your heart, and life, since becoming consistently thankful to God? Has He started to lead you in a new direction? Journal your thoughts.*

*2. Does your life reflect being an ambassador for Christ? Has the Lord begun to reveal areas of your life that need to be renewed? Write them down. Read Hebrews 6:1–12. Thank God for giving you "faith and patience" to inherit every promise He has for you, and for your divine destiny. Write down what happens after you quiet yourself before Him in prayer.*

*3. Since you have started following God's pattern of prayer, have any "natural elements," like anger, gossip, difficult circumstances, etc., hindered you from spending time with God and going deeper in the Word? Take these*

*experiences to God, ask Him for wisdom (for each one),*

*and then lay your burdens at His feet. Write down what you receive from Him in prayer, and begin to move forward again.*

*4. Are you stuck in the "praise section" of prayer? Do you keep slipping back into sin? Go and "confess your fault" to a "righteous" man or woman (like your pastor...), so that God can deliver you, and get you back on course in prayer. Write in your journal about this experience, and thank God for His faithfulness.*

*5. Are you starting to see and experience the results of consistent prayer? Look back in your journal to when you began. Let God lead you through the pages, then write what He revealed to you on this journey.*

*6. Are you ready to leave the elementary things of God? Are you ready undergo the first stage of preparation for intercessory prayer? Update your list of things that (God has revealed) need to change in your heart and life. Read the Bible and find out what it says concerning these areas; ask God to lead you to the Brazen Laver.*

# THINK OF THAT

**The Outer Court The Early Stages of Prayer Ex. 27:9–15**

SELAH

# Chapter Three

## THE BRAZEN LAVER: THE PLACE OF WASHING

As you go deeper into the Outer Court, just passed the Brazen Altar, you encounter the first stage in this third step of the pattern of prayer—the Brazen Laver. Let me review. You have passed through the Gate that represents the 4 works of Jesus Christ: His righteousness, divinity (coming down from heaven to earth), kingship, and His ultimate sacrifice on the Cross. As He draws you deeper into His presence, you begin to experience the manifestation of these works—so you enter His courts in prayer, every day, praising and thanking God for what He has already done.

The Brazen Laver is the first place God will lead you in prayer. It represents the first piece of furniture in the Tabernacle, and the first part of God's nature that begins to embrace your life. It is your first stage of preparation to become an intercessor. Exodus 30:19–21 says,

**"For Aaron and his sons shall wash their hands and their feet thereat: when they go into the tabernacle of the congregation, they shall wash with water that they die not; or when they come near to the altar to minister, to burn offering made by fire unto the Lord: so shall they wash their hands and their feet, that they die not..."**

All priests were required to wash before performing any ministry-function, so this tells us that prayer is not supposed to stay on the personal level. You are to pass through the "personal level" of prayer through the cleansing, so that you can begin to pray for others. If you are thinking, "I am not a priest." Think again. You are a priest, and if you are saved, God is going to begin a work in you that starts at the Brazen Laver.

**"So be done with every trace of wickedness (depravity, malignity) and all deceit and insincerity (pretense, hypocrisy) and grudges (envy, jealousy) and slander and evil speaking of every kind. Like newborn babies you should crave (thirst for, earnestly desire) the pure (unadulterated) spiritual milk, that by it you may be nurtured and grow unto [completed] salvation, since you have [already] tasted the goodness and kindness of the Lord. Come to Him [then, to**

**that] Living Stone which men tried and threw away, but which is chosen [and] precious in God's sight. [Come] and, like living stones, be yourselves built [into] a spiritual house, for a holy (dedicated, consecrated) priesthood, to offer up [those] spiritual sacrifices [that are] acceptable and pleasing to God through Jesus Christ."**
**1 Peter 2:1–5, (AMP)**

In other words, you have already tasted the goodness of God (through salvation) at the Gate, so now you are a priest—and God is about to dedicate and consecrate you unto Him. Unlike the five-fold ministry gifts in Ephesians 4:11 (i.e., apostle, prophet, evangelist, pastor, and teacher), prayer has been given to "all men." You do not have to function in the five-fold ministry to pray. You are a priest, and no matter what you do in the church, or how old you are in Christ, God has called you to pray, every day. Luke 18:1 says,

**"...men ought always to pray, and not to faint..."**

Since prayer is not just a personal relationship with God, but also a ministry, before you can minister on any level— to yourself, someone else, or unto the Lord—you have to wash first. You cannot minister unless you have been "prepared" by God. Ephesians 5:22–27 says,

**"Wives, be subject (be submissive and adapt yourselves) to your own husbands as [a service] to the Lord. For the husband is head of the wife as Christ is the Head of the church, Himself the Savior of [His] body. As the church is subject to Christ, so let wives also be subject in everything to their husbands. Husbands, love your wives, as Christ loved the church and gave Himself up for her, so that He might sanctify her, having cleansed her by the washing of water with the Word, that He might present the church to Himself in glorious splendor, without spot or wrinkle or any such things [that she might be holy and faultless]."**
**(AMP)**

In the natural, this is speaking to husbands and wives, but in the Spirit realm, it paints a picture of the cleansing every believer must undergo as the bride of Christ. Jesus gave up His life so that we would be sanctified, "…having cleansed her by the washing of water with the Word."

So as soon as you get into the Outer Court, the Lord is going to lead you straight to the Brazen

Laver because He has already given Himself up so that you could be made righteous.

As you wash, you are stripping off the "old (unregenerate) self"—your flesh—according to Colossians 3:9 (AMP), which cannot go to the next level of prayer. John 6:63 says,

**"It is the Spirit Who gives life [He is the Life-giver]; the flesh conveys no benefit whatever [there is no profit in it]. The words (truths) that I have been speaking to you are spirit and life."**
**(AMP)**

This is why the Old Testament priests never burned the "flesh" of a sacrifice on the altar! If you read through Leviticus 8 and 9, you will see that they always burned the flesh "outside the camp." So by washing at the laver, you are taking off the old covering, so that you will be able to put on the "new" clothing that God is going to give you in Chapter 5.

The Brazen Laver is where God begins to manifest His works in you—so the outer layer must come off.

## A PERFECT CONSTRUCTION

In the Tabernacle, there were items that had been made from wood (representing humanity), and then overlaid in either bronze, or gold. Other items were made from solid gold. The Brazen Laver was made from solid bronze, which is a "type" of the judgment of God. He is the final judge of whether or not we are truly clean. So while we wash at the laver, the brass also reminds us that there is a judgment for those who reject the Word, who reject the cleansing. John 5:22 says, "Even the Father judges no one, for He has given all judgment (the last judgment and the whole business of judging) entirely into the hands of the Son."**(AMP)**

Remember, Jesus is the Word "...made flesh..." Jn.1:14

The laver was the only item in the Outer Court that had no measurements. Since there was no

wood in its construction, it represented the unlimited ability of God's
Word to wash and cleanse us.

It does not matter how far you have fallen, or what you have done. When you get to the Brazen Laver, it is able to wash you clean.

Nothing is too deep for the laver to cleanse, too far in your past to erase, or too far into your future to control. The laver's cleansing power is unlimited so you can become exactly what God has destined for you to be, and you can be "fitly cleansed and prepared" to become an intercessor.

## A PERFECT REFLECTION

Another part of the Brazen Laver's construction can be found in Exodus 38:8,

**"He made the laver and its base of bronze from the mirrors of the women who ministered at the door of the Tent of Meeting."**
**(AMP)**

I think it is interesting, and somewhat cute, that women provided the mirrors, because the spirit of vanity is portrayed more in women, than in men. It is almost like God moved upon these women to surrender this vanity, therefore, overcoming it. In a general sense, I believe this represents a surrendering of what you think you look like to the Lord. Do you really know what "manner of man" you are?

When a priest approached the Brazen Laver, he not only saw a reflection of himself in the water, he saw a second reflection in the basin. There could be no mistake about how he looked. When you go to the Brazen Laver in prayer, God will show you a reflection of who you are, but also—because you have come to Him—He will also reflect the Word into your life. He will begin the process of "completing" your salvation, according to 1 Peter 2:1–

5. (AMP)

This is where you become conscious of "doing" the

Word that God "reflects" to you from that basin—where you make the decision to start living for God, and become a true reflection of Him. It is where you make the decision to rise up from your prayer closet and walk out what you believe. James 1:22–25 says,

**"But be doers of the Word [obey the message], and not merely listeners to it, betraying yourselves [into deception by reasoning contrary to the Truth]. For if anyone also listens to the Word without obeying it and being a doer of it, he is like a man who looks carefully at his [own] natural face in a mirror; [remember the mirrored bronze?] for he thoughtfully observes himself, and then goes off and promptly forgets what he was like. But he who looks carefully into the faultless law, [the Word of God], the [law] of liberty, and is faithful to it and perseveres in looking into it, being not a heedless listener who forgets but an active doer [who obeys], he shall be blessed in his doing (his life of obedience)."**
**(AMP)**

In other words, when you stop to wash, you are not only "beholding" what you look like, you are at the place where you can do something about what you see. The two-fold function of the Brazen Laver is powerful. The Word allows you to see yourself as you really are, and it helps you to obey the revealed Word. You behold yourself through the water of the Word, while it washes off the things that need to be cleansed according to John 15:3, "Now ye are clean through the word which I have spoken unto you."

Remember that you must accept the grace to obey what God has revealed, or you will "forget" and lose your blessings.

Many people hear the Word, but do not perceive that they need to "do" what it says. They hang around in the Outer Court, and then wander over to the Brazen Laver to wash—because "everybody else is doing it." They say, "This is just something that I am supposed to do." These believers cannot endure the washing, so they run away from the laver to a place where they feel more " comfortable."

Many times, these people have come to God because they thought they were "supposed to want to be saved." They also think that God is supposed to answer their prayers, even though they constantly break His pattern.

If only they would submit to the washing at the Brazen Laver! It has the power to reveal the truth about who they really are, by casting a reflection that would cause them to understand—we are not only supposed to wash, we need to wash. We are lost without the 4 works of Christ in salvation, and we cannot go deeper in God unless we first stop and wash at the Brazen Laver!

If this describes you, then you probably look for a demand (proof of something) before you admit that you need help from God. Is your life so perfect now that you cannot see how Christ—the Lord of glory, the King of kings, the Word made flesh—could improve your to

human condition? Are you afraid that you are going to lose something that you deeply desire? Go to the Brazen Laver. It can expose sin and deception to the degree that you will see, beyond the shadow of a doubt, you need to change. You need to submit to the washing.

## A PERFECT COMMUNION

Let us go to Hebrews 4:12-14,

**"For the word that God speaks is alive and full of power [making it active, operative, energizing, and effective]; it is sharper than any two-edged sword, penetrating to the dividing line of the breath of**

**life (soul) and [the immortal] spirit, and of joints and marrow [of the deepest parts of our nature], exposing and sifting and analyzing and judging the very thoughts and purposes of the heart. And nota**
**creature exists that is concealed from His sight, but all things are open and exposed, naked and defenseless to the eyes of Him with Whom we have to do. Inasmuch then as we have a great High Priest Who has[already] ascended and passed through the heavens, Jesus the Son of God, let us hold fast our confession [of faith in Him]."**
**(AMP)**

Jesus, our High Priest, has already walked through every stage of intercession. We must follow Him, since we are a royal priesthood, and joint-heirs with Him. In our priestly duties, we have to walk through all of the stages in prayer, just like He did. It is another form of "communion." Like the bread and wine, Jesus' body has already been broken, and His blood has already been shed for us. Yet as often as we "do" our priestly duty of prayer, in remembrance of Him, we demonstrate the works that He has already done.

1 Cor. 11:26

So "as often as we do" this priestly duty, since we still live in this fleshly realm…we have to come before Him consistently, every day, in this form of communion. By doing this, we reaffirm where we are, and where we desire to be. We have to wash, and let the Word of God cleanse us, before we can move to the next stage of following Christ; going to the Brazen Altar. If we are to use the two-edged Sword against the enemy, we must first wash and let it divide the line between our soul and spirit, to the deepest parts of our being.

## YOU CANNOT STAY AT THE LAVER

Remember, if you stay at the Brazen Laver, the only person that you will be able to pray for is you. Outer Court prayer focuses on self; what you are doing wrong, what you are limited in, how you have failed, what you need to overcome, what you need to be encouraged in, what you need to be cleansed from, etc. In the Outer Court, it is all about YOU. God will always deal with you before He will use you to intercede for others.

As long as you remain satisfied praying only for yourself, and everything is still about you, then you have not obeyed God and gone on to intercession. You are still in the elementary level of prayer. You are not supposed to stay here, you are supposed to pass through this realm into a deeper walk with God.

So this first stage (of the third step) in God's pattern of prayer is about you getting cleansed and prepared to be purified. The priests had to wash at the Brazen Laver every day, so there should not be one day that you do not wash in the Word! You are part of the royal priesthood of God, which means that washing in prayer is a requirement: you do not wash one day, and skip the next day. The Old Testament priests could not skip days in their duties!
Once they were ordained and chosen by God to be priests, it was their lifestyle until they died.

You cannot afford to miss one day in prayer, because if you do, then you cancel the pattern of God. You cancel the pattern of the body of Christ. You interfere with something God has set into place. Whether you realize it or not, you are trying to change the pattern of heaven, and that is ignoring the work of our Savior. You are bypassing Jesus Christ and going straight to God the Father, when He said, "...no man cometh unto the Father, but by Me." [Jn 14:6] Have you really reached the throne of God, or have you tapped into a "familiar" zone that the enemy has planted in the spirit realm, to make you believe that you are tapping God?

Remember, Ephesians 2:2 says that Satan is the "prince of the power of the air." He controls the atmosphere, and that familiar spirit can make you think that you are tapping God, when you have not gone by "the way." Remember the pattern? "I am the way, the truth, and the life…" So if you skip "the way", you definitely have not arrived at "the truth", and you certainly have not reached "the life", which is the "…light of men."

This is the pattern God has established to prepare you for intercessory prayer.

Now do you see why it is not important that we simply pray? It is important that we pray correctly, because we are praying to get results. You will also see, as we progress through this mini-book series, that at every step in God's pattern of prayer: from the Outer Court, to the Holy Place, and into the Most Holy Place…the Word will always be there.

You cannot have a successful, effective prayer life without the Word of God.

**The Brazen Laver The Place of Washing Ex. 30:19–21**

*1. Have you continued to read the Bible every day, especially the books of John, Romans, and Genesis? Have you looked up the scriptures that pertain to the areas God wants you to change in your life? Write down in your journal how God has begun to "wash" your life through His Word (start to record your spiritual testimonies).*

*2. When you read the Word, are there certain scriptures that "stick out" to you? If so, stop and meditate on these verses and find others on the same topic. Write down what you are learning from "searching" God's Word.*

*3. Are your thoughts and feelings changing about habits, circumstances, and/or people in your life? Is God dealing with you to make some changes? If so, ask Him how you should begin. As He prompts you through this process, write each step down in your journal. Then look back and see if a pattern is developing.*

*4. Have "traces of wickedness" surfaced within you during this time of washing? If so, let God show you how to deal with it. As they come to the surface, give them to God (in repentance), ask Him to "create a clean heart" in you, and to "renew" your spirit. Forgive yourself. Ask others to forgive you. Confess and be healed. Write your testimony, and then get up and start washing again.*

*5. Are you starting to see a "new you," as God reflects who you really are through the Brazen Laver? Write down the things He prompts you to do, and record every victory, so that you can trace the pattern and walk in it, over and over again.*

*6. As you "hold fast your confession," according to Hebrews 4:12–14, are you learning how to speak the Word into your own life? Are you practicing how to say nothing, when you recognize that the words are coming from your earthly nature? Are you learning how to hold the spiritual truths God is teaching you in prayer, until (and if) He tells you to release them? Study about the "tongue" in God's Word. Record your journey.*

*7. Are you praying every day, at the time God has directed? Are you obeying Him throughout the day, praying whenever He prompts you to pray—even if it is for just a few minutes, or less? Are you ready to surrender your will to God at the Brazen Altar?*

**The Brazen Laver The Place of Washing Ex. 30:19–21**

______________________________________________

______________________________________________

______________________________________________

______________________________________________

______________________________________________

______________________________________________

______________________________________________

______________________________________________

______________________________________________

______________________________________________

______________________________________________

______________________________________________

# Chapter Four

## THE BRAZEN ALTAR: THE PLACE OF SACRIFICE

Once you have washed at the Brazen Laver, acknowledging everything that God has shown you is displeasing to Him, it is time to be purified at the Brazen Altar. This is the second stage (of the third step in God's pattern of prayer), where you let go of your will, and embrace what God desires. Infant prayer says, "Give me this, give me that." The prayer of sacrifice says, "God, I surrender to your will. Whatever You want, I want. Yes, Lord!"

So you have entered through the Gate of the works of Jesus Christ with thanksgiving and praise, you have submitted to the "washing of the Word" at the Brazen Laver, and now you know exactly what you look like and what "manner of man" you are. You have come through "the way," but you are still in the realm of personal prayer. You have not gotten to the level of "truth," where you will make intercession for others, because your Outer

Court experience is not complete. You must be broken before the Lord.

The Outer Court experience must be "inclusive"— you must pass through every stage—or your prayers will be limited to the realm of the Outer Court, YOU.

## WHAT IS AN ALTAR?

The word, "altar," means a "slaughter" place. Strong's 4196 & 2076, Heb. In the Greek, it is called "a place of sacrifice." Strong's 2379, 2378 & 2380 The Brazen Altar is the place where the things of the flesh—bad and good— are burned up by the all-consuming fire of God. It is the stage where you become a "living sacrifice," according to Romans 12:1–3.

**"I appeal to you therefore, brethren, and beg of you in view of [all] the mercies of God, to make a decisive dedication of your bodies [presenting all your members and faculties] as a living sacrifice, holy (devoted, consecrated) and well pleasing to God, which is your reasonable (rational, intelligent) service and spiritual worship. Do not be conformed to this world**

**(this age), [fashioned after and adapted to its external, superficial customs], but be transformed (changed) by the [entire] renewal of your mind [by its new ideals and its new attitude], so that you may prove [for yourselves] what is the good and acceptable and perfect will of God, even the thing which is good and acceptable and perfect [in His sight for you]. For by the grace (unmerited favor of God) given to me I warn everyone among you not to estimate and think of himself more highly than he ought [not to have an exaggerated opinion of his own importance], but to rate his ability with sober judgment, each according to the degree of faith apportioned by God to him."**
**(AMP)**

Remember, you are a priest unto God, a member of the "royal priesthood" of Christ. You must be washed, and you must undergo the fire of consecration. This is the place where you take the "new ideals and attitude" you received at the Brazen Laver to the next level—proving that you will submit to God's perfect will for your life— body, soul, and spirit. Otherwise, how can God use you to make intercession for others?

## A SOUND CONSTRUCTION

God told Moses in Exodus 27:1–8,

**"And make the altar of acacia wood, five cubits square and three cubits high [within reach of all]. Make horns for it on its four corners; they shall be of one piece with it, and you shall overlay it with bronze. You shall make pots to take away its ashes, and shovels, basins, forks, and firepans; make all its utensils of bronze. Also make for it a grate, a network of bronze; and on the net you shall make four bronze rings at its four corners. And you shall put it under the ledge of the altar, so that the net will extend halfway down the altar. And make poles for the altar, poles of acacia wood overlaid with bronze. The poles shall be put through the rings on the two sides of the altar, with which to carry it. You shall make [the altar] hollow with slabs or planks; as shown you on the mountain, so shall it be made."**
**(AMP)**

Let me encourage you. Five is the number of grace, and three represents the godhead. So when you go to the Brazen Altar, you are submitting to (proving) the work of the godhead…so you will be "transformed" by the grace of God! Though you must come to the Brazen Altar on God's terms, you are by no means alone. Jesus is already in the fire (perfecting it), so He will be with you…just like He was with Shadrach, Meshach, and Abednego. [Dan. 3:24–25] (Let me remind you that they were not "consumed" in the fire, and God was with them, because they had refused to serve and worship other gods. [Dan. 3:12] We will study this more deeply in the next volume.)

The Brazen Altar was formed out of wood, and then overlaid in bronze. This means it had to be measured, because wood represents humanity; and whenever humanity is involved, there are limitations. The bronze signifies judgment, so God established the Brazen Altar as the place of blood sacrifice, where the blood of Christ would make the final atonement for the limitations of man! The priests slaughtered the sacrificial lambs at the Brazen Altar, and Jesus is the Lamb that was slain, according to Isaiah 53:5–7,

**"But He was wounded for our transgressions, He was bruised for our guilt and iniquities; the chastisement [needful to obtain] peace and well-being for us was upon Him, and with the stripes [that wounded] Him we are healed and made whole. All we like sheep have gone astray, we have turned everyone to his own way; and the Lord has made to light upon Him the guilt and iniquity of us all. He was oppressed, [yet when] He was afflicted, He was submissive and opened not His mouth; like a lamb that is led to the slaughter, and as a sheep before her shearers is dumb, so He opened not His mouth."**
**(AMP)**

Jesus Christ was placed upon the wood of sacrifice. He went under the fire, and died on the Cross. He is the Lamb that was slain from the foundation of the world Rev. 13:8, the final sacrifice, and He did not open His mouth. How much more, when we approach the Brazen Altar, should we learn to keep our mouths shut? Many believers fail the test in this area, and then we have to go back and wash our mouths out with holy water! When you become a "living sacrifice," you have to learn how to be silent before God, and everybody else.

God is saying, "You must daily put

yourself on the Brazen Altar in prayer, because if you do not put your flesh on the altar, and if you do not offer yourself up as a sacrifice, then you will be limited in what you can do for Me." There is always a sacrifice before service.

Let me encourage you again. When Jesus was crucified, "...and they saw that He was already dead, they did not break His legs. But one of the soldiers pierced His side with a spear, and immediately blood and water came (flowed) out." Jn. 19:33–34, (AMP) Not only did this prove Jesus was the Messiah, according to Exodus 12:46, Numbers 9:12, Psalm 34:20, and Zechariah 12:10, it sealed the work of the Brazen Laver (water) and the Brazen Altar (blood). What else does God have to say to confirm His process of prayer?

Many people are serving God in the sanctuary, preaching, praying, prophesying, laying on hands, but have not yet passed by the Brazen Altar! They have not stopped at the place of sacrifice and given all to God, they have not given up their will. Look at Jesus in the Garden of Gethsemane; that is exactly what He did. The Bible says that He prayed until "His sweat became like great clots of blood dropping down upon the ground." Lk. 22:44, (AMP) He laid down His will. That is why He said, "…Father, if you are willing, remove this cup from Me; yet not My will, but [always] Yours be done." Lk. 22:42 (AMP)

In the realm of the Spirit, Jesus had made it to the Brazen Altar. He laid Himself on that altar and said, "In My flesh, I do not want to do this. I cannot do this… nevertheless…I want what You want. Yes, Father! I am not going to let the limitations of My flesh keep Me from the supernatural operation of My spirit." Mark 10:45 confirms, "For even the Son of Man came not to have service rendered to Him, but to serve, and to give His life as a ransom for (instead of) many." (AMP)

Before we can operate in the Spirit realm, before we can operate in prayer, we must stop by the Brazen Altar. We must pray, "God, whatever it is, I lay it down. Whatever my will is, whatever my thoughts are…" As we sacrifice our will in prayer, then eternal life—through Christ's ultimate sacrifice—fills our being.

**"For we do not have a High Priest Who is unableto understand and sympathize and have a shared feeling with our weaknesses and infirmities and liability to the assaults of temptation, but One Who has been tempted in every respect as we are, yet without sinning."**
**Hebrews 4:15, (AMP)**

Too many times, we come before God in prayer for others, but we are praying from the Outer Court. Let me give you clarity today, from the Holy Ghost, if you have not gone into the Holy Place and the Most Holy Place, the only person you can pray for in the Outer Court is YOU. You are not in intercession yet! You are still in self-sacrifice. You are still laying down your ideas, and your will, at the altar of God.

For example, if you are praying for a loved one from the Outer Court, and you have a way that you want it to go, then you take it to prayer without stopping by the Brazen Altar (giving up your will)—then you are trying to enter the Throne room of God telling Him what to do! Instead, you should be saying, "Lord, let Thy will be done."

Church, we are not praying according to

the will of God. You pray, "God, do something with Junior...he is on my last nerve. God, if you are not going to save him, just kill him, just do whatever You have to do..." What kind of prayer is that? God has not told you to pray for people "by any means necessary." So Junior gets into an accident and loses an eye...now you have to lead him around! You cannot complain, because that is what YOU prayed! Listen to me. You have to sacrifice yourself at the Brazen Altar before God can use you in intercession. Otherwise, you will "sacrifice" everybody else at the altar of your will!

When you let go of your will, and put yourself on the Brazen Altar, you will get to the second and the third realms by receiving the will, mind, knowledge, and illumination of God. You will not carry your thoughts, ways, and ideas before His throne—you receive His knowledge and revelation as you enter into intercession. As long as you stay in the Outer Court, on the Brazen Altar, you only can pray for you. This is why you must go beyond Outer Court prayer, through self-sacrifice, to intercession in the Holy Place. You cannot stay in the Outer Court.

## AN EQUAL SACRIFICE

Do you remember that the Brazen Altar was 3 cubits high? This matches the measurements of the Ark of the Covenant. The base of the Ark was 2½ cubits, but when they molded and mounted the cherubim on top, it was also 3 cubits high. This means the glory of God will be equal to the sacrifice you make on the Brazen Altar. If there is no communion here, there will be no connection in the Most Holy Place. If you want to have power in prayer, then your sacrifice must measure up to that level

**"So that, [just] as sin has reigned in death, [so] grace (His unearned and undeserved favor) might reign also through righteousness (right standing with God) which issues in eternal life through Jesus Christ (the Messiah, the Anointed One) our Lord. What shall we say [to all this]? Are we to remain in sin in order that God's grace (favor and mercy) may multiply and overflow? Certainly not! How can we who have died to sin live in it any longer? Are you ignorant of the fact that all of us who have been baptized into Christ Jesus were baptized into His death? We were buried therefore with Him by the baptism into death, so that just as Christ was raised from the dead by the glorious [power] of the Father, so we too might [habitually] live and behave in newness of life. For if we have become one with Him by sharing a deathlike His, we shall also be [one with Him in sharing] His resurrection [by a new life lived for God]."**
**Romans 5:21–6:5, (AMP)**

Too many believers are trying to get greater power with little sacrifice. We do not want to give up anything on the Brazen Altar. We do not want to sacrifice, or die, to anything! We do not want to submit to anything, we do not want to give up living in sin—but we want everything that God has in the third dimension of prayer. We will never get it, because this is "ignoring" the works of Christ, and disregarding the pattern of God! The danger is, you think that you are in the light of God, but you are still in natural light, because you are still in the Outer Court.

Just as daylight leaves and night comes, sometimes you can see your way, and sometimes you cannot. Sometimes you see that you have the victory, and sometimes you cannot.

Selah, stop and think about that.

This is why you shout for the victory saying, "I am on my way, I can make it," and then other times, you cannot see your way out of a hat. You are in the Outer Court. You have to wait until the sun comes up again. You have to wait until the natural senses kick in; you have to wait to get your paycheck to "see" that your bills are paid. You always have to wait for the earthly elements to know that you have the victory.

In the third realm, the light is supernatural. It always shines forth, because it is lit by the Shekinah glory of God, so we always have victory in the third dimension of prayer! How do I know this? How can we know this is the pattern of God? Let us go to the Word of God in Leviticus 9:23– 24, that tells what took place after Moses had consecrated Aaron, and Aaron had made the first sacrifices for the children of Israel,

**"Moses and Aaron went into the Tent of Meeting,and when they came out they blessed the people, and the glory of the Lord [the Shekinah cloud] appeared to all the people [as promised]. Then there came a fire out from before the Lord and consumed the burnt offering and the fat on the altar; and when all the people saw it, they shouted and fell on their faces."**
**(AMP)**

At this solemn assembly, after seven days of consecration had been completed for Aaron and his sons, the glory of God came down into the Most Holy Place; and this divine fire shot forth from the third realm, and kindled upon the sacrifices on the Brazen Altar. So the original flame that lit the Brazen Altar came directly from heaven! This fire was to burn "continually."

Do you see the pattern? Aaron performed the sacrifices according to the pattern God had revealed to Moses. Lev. 1–8 When he made the sacrifices the right way—according to God's will—when the correct weight of sacrifice was there, God consumed it. After this "day of obedience" to God, the priests were to make sure that fire never went out. Leviticus 6:12–13 says,

**"And the fire upon the altar shall be kept burning on it; it shall not be allowed to go out. The priest shall burn wood on it every morning and lay the burnt offering in order upon it and he shall burn on it the fat of the peace offerings. The fire shall be burning continually upon the altar; it shall not go out."**
**(AMP)**

Remember that wood represents humanity, which means that we are required, every single day, to lay ourselves on the Brazen Altar and say, "God, whatever is not pleasing to You, burn it up. Consume it—my will, desires, emotions—anything that is out of Your will." We have become the wood that is on that altar, keeping God's fire lit. Continuously.

## THE HORNS OF HELP

In its construction, the Brazen Altar had four horns, one on each corner, which represent salvation, strength, and power. So when you lay yourself on the Brazen Altar of sacrifice, you receive salvation, strength, and power to do the will of God. You gain the ability to be resilient in prayer, and strong in intercession. In other words, when you go into the Holy Place, you will not be in intercession for somebody else, all the while doubting your own walk. The battle is over once you receive God's will on the Brazen Altar! Luke 1:68-69 says,

**"Blessed (praised and extolled and thanked) be the Lord, the God of Israel, because He has come and brought deliverance and redemption to His people! And He has raised up a Horn of salvation [a mighty and valiant Helper, the Author of salvation] for us in the house of David His servant..."**
**(AMP)**

God has raised up the "Horn of salvation" as a mighty, and valiant Helper! Many times, then, the missing ingredient in our prayers is salvation! This is why many prayers are not being answered, because salvation is one of the horns on the Brazen Altar. Salvation helps us while we pray.

How in the world are you going to make intercession without any help from God? How did you walk past your Helper, slip under the white linen curtain on the side of the wall, and sneak into the Most Holy Place, thinking that you are going to receive something from Him?

You do not have your Helper! How did you even manage to get in the Door and beyond the veil without the blood sacrifice?

The enemy has deceived us.

You cannot pray effectively if you are ignoring the works of Christ! The process of "completing" our salvation begins at the Brazen Laver, and it is sealed by the finished work of Christ—the lamb who was slain before the foundation of the world—on the Brazen Altar.

Since the horns represent salvation, strength, and power, then the blood of Jesus is that power, which can "perfect" your sacrifice there. The number 4 represents the earth and its elements—the 4 winds and 4 corners of the earth—so Christ's redeeming blood is u n l i m i t e d in its power. (This also ties in to the Golden Altar in the Holy Place, which you will learn about in the next book.) Romans 11:22 says,

**"Then note and appreciate the gracious kindness and the severity of God: severity toward those who have fallen, but God's gracious kindness to you—provided you continue in His grace and abide in His kindness; otherwise you too will be cut off (pruned away)."**
**(AMP)**

**"For the time [has arrived] for judgment to begin with the household of God; and if it begins with us, what will [be] the end of those who do not respect or believe or obey the good news (the Gospel) of God?**
**And if the righteous are barely saved, what will become of the godless and wicked?"**
**1 Peter 4:17–18, (AMP)**

This is why we must "work out" our own

salvation, according to Philippians 2:9–13,

**"Therefore [because He stooped so low] God has highly exalted Him and has freely bestowed on Him the name that is above every name, that in (at) the name of Jesus every knee should (must) bow, in heaven and on earth and under the earth, and every tongue [frankly and openly] confess and acknowledge that Jesus Christ is Lord, to the glory of God the Father. Therefore, my dear ones, as you have always obeyed [my suggestions], so now, not only [with the enthusiasm you would show] in my presence but much more because I am absent, work out (cultivate, carry out to the goal, and fully complete) your own salvation with reverence and awe and trembling (self-distrust, with serious caution, tenderness of conscience, watchfulness against temptation, timidly shrinking from whatever might offend God and discredit the name of Christ). [Not in your own strength] for it is God Who is all the while effectually at work in you [energizing and creating in you the power and desire], both to will and to work for His good pleasure and satisfaction and delight."**
**(AMP)**

Do you see the revelation? Our Help, to lay on that altar and complete the process of salvation, in order to snatch others from the flames, is in the name of Jesus—our salvation! Fear of God will keep you on that altar…and it will keep you humble when you go into the Holy Place and make intercession for others. Otherwise, when God answers your prayers (that you pray according to His will), you will become proud and forget "the name" that put the horns of salvation, strength, and power on that altar of sacrifice. Let us continue in Romans 1:16,

**"For I am not ashamed of the Gospel (good news) of Christ, for it is God's power working unto salvation [for deliverance from eternal death] to everyone who believes with a personal trust and a confident surrender and firm reliance, to the Jew first and also to the Greek. For in the Gospel, a righteousness which God ascribes is revealed, both springing from faith and leading to faith [disclosed through the way of faith that arouses to more faith] ..."**
**(AMP)**

This is the reason why we do not believe half of what we are asking God to do in prayer. "The way" that God leads and arouses us—from faith to faith—through the horns on the Brazen Altar, which is our salvation. Romans 1:17 concludes by saying,

**"...As it is written, The man who through faith is just and upright shall live and shall live by faith."**
**(AMP)**

Let me tie this together...you come through the Gate (of the 4 works of Christ) at salvation, but faith to "do" His works comes at the Brazen Altar. It comes supernaturally when you lay your will down on the altar of sacrifice, and grab hold of the horns of the altar. You lay down y o u r will and desires, and you pick up a completed salvation; you pick up the Helper that gives you faith to be a "living sacrifice." You pick up the One that is going to help you at every level of intercession.

Salvation always defeats the enemy! In the book of Joshua, chapter 6, the children of Israel marched around the walls of Jericho, and blew the trumpet. (In those days, a ram's horn was used as a trumpet, which represents salvation...a Helper.) Verse 20 says that when the Israelites heard the trumpet, they "raised a great shout," and the wall of Jericho fell to the ground. (AMP) When people hear their Helper, they can see the enemy falling...*need I say more?*

Let us go to Genesis 22:2 & 9, when God required Abraham to offer up Isaac, his

only son. He was calling Abraham to break tradition, go against his own will, and sacrifice on an altar that he would build himself. Abraham had to exemplify the very act of God—which would cut the new covenant by offering up His "only begotten Son" as a sacrifice for the world. Jn. 3:16 When he obeyed God at that altar of sacrifice, Abraham completed the process that confirmed his new name…the "father of many nations."
Gen. 17.4, (AMP)

Genesis 22:13 says that Abraham glanced around and, "…behold, behind him was a ram caught in a thicket by his horns. And Abraham went and took the ram and offered it up for a burnt offering and an ascending sacrifice instead of his son!" (AMP) Abraham got his helper out of the bushes…after he had put his son on the altar. He laid down his desire, and reaped the nations through the horns of salvation! Let us read another example in 1 Kings 1:46– 53,

**"Solomon sits on the royal throne. Moreover, the king's servants came over to congratulate our Lord, King David, saying, May God make the name of Solomon better than your name and make his throne greater than your throne. And the king bowed himself upon the bed and said, Blessed be the Lord, the God of Israel, Who has granted me to see one of my offspring sitting on my throne this day. And all the guests that were with Adonijah were afraid and rose up and went every man his way. And Adonijah feared because of Solomon, and arose and went [to the tabernacle tent on Mt. Zion] and caught hold of the horns of the altar [as a fugitive's refuge]. And it was told Solomon, Behold Adonijah fears King Solomon, for behold, he has caught hold of the horns of the altar, saying, Let King Solomon swear to me first that he will not slay his servant with the sword. Solomon said, If he will show himself to be a worthy man, not a hair on him shall fall to the ground; but if wickedness is found in him, he shall die. So King Solomon sent, and they brought Adonijah down from the altar [in front of the tabernacle]. He came and bowed himself to King Solomon, and Solomon said to him, Go to your house."**
**(AMP)**

Why was Adonijah saved? He grabbed hold of the horns of the altar—his Help! When Adonijah feared for his life, he grabbed the horns…he threw himself on the altar of sacrifice.

*There is power in throwing yourself on the altar, and there is greater power—a continuous fire—when you keep yourself there.*

You see, God lit the fire on the Brazen Altar, but the priest used this same fire to light the Golden Candlestick and Altar of Incense in the Holy Place! In other words, the "fires" of intercession will be equal to your sacrifice on the Brazen Altar. Your life keeps the fire burning. If you do not keep yourself on the altar, like fresh wood that is laid upon it daily, the fire will go out. If the fire goes out, you will not have any "illumination" of God's Word (which is in the Holy Place across from the Golden Candlestick, but we will get to that later).

Without illumination of God's Word through sacrifice, you cannot make intercession. Your level of sacrifice determines the depth and weight of your worship, and the spiritual insight that you receive from the

Word of God. Now let me ask, what are you willing to put on the Brazen Altar, and give up toGod?

## BEWARE OF STRANGE FIRE

Now turn with me to Leviticus 10:1–3,

**"And Nadab and Abihu, the sons of Aaron, each took his censer and put fire in it, and put incense on it,and offered strange and unholy fire before the Lord, as He had not commanded them. And there came forth fire from before the Lord and killed them, and they died before the Lord. Then Moses said to Aaron, This is what the Lord meant when He said, I [and My will, not their own] will be acknowledged as hallowed by those who come near Me, and before all the people I will be honored. And Aaron said nothing."**
**(AMP)**

This is why the work of the sanctuary is tainted in our time. There are "images" of worship, praise, altars, sanctification, and holiness, but we are denying the power thereof. 2 Tim. 3:5 We are ignoring the pattern—the original requirements to enter God's presence—which explains why many in Christendom are operating in "strange fire."

I believe this is the reason so much "strange worship" is going around—people singing worldly songs, and songs that identify with the world and carnal worship—because they have not sanctified their wills on the altar. Like Nadab and Abihu, they have taken their own censers, their own lives, put their own incense in them, and lit them up. They have their own personal mixture, and they call it worship.

God is saying all the while, "I did not light that fire. That is not the fire from the altar of sacrifice."

If you do not sacrifice anything, you are just lighting a fire. You need to understand that, before God lit the fire in the Brazen Altar in Leviticus 9:24, it had already been lit. This was "in order" with God's plan…because that was all they knew. [Lev. 6:9–13 & 8, (AMP)] When the real fire came from God, in the 9th chapter, then the man-made fire was no longer acceptable. God had replaced it.

God replaces your fire with the fire of purification. Death and destruction come to those who, afterwards, keep lighting their own fire.

Could this be the reason why we do not pray with fervor? Could this be why our prayers are not "effectual"? Could this be the reason that our prayers are not "availing" much?

Strange fires are everywhere in Christendom today. That is why we are serving the Lord, and are still in slavery to our flesh. We are doing what we want to do, acting and reacting according to our emotions, *and we have lit our own fire.* Is your flesh stirred up? That is your fire…not God's. Galatians 5:17 says,

**"For the desires of the flesh are opposed to the[Holy] Spirit, and [desires of the] Spirit are opposed to the flesh (godless human nature) …"**
**(AMP)**

Which means, if you do not put your will on the Brazen Altar, you will get inside of the Holy Place fighting God with your flesh, instead of making intercession. God will say to you, "Turn left." You will say, "Well, I feel led in my spirit to go right." God will say, "I want you to stay right here and pray some more for Sister

Watermelon." You will say, "Well, I feel kind-of thirsty..." He will respond, "No, I do not want you to drink yet, I want you to keep..." "But God, I just want to get some juice..." "No, I want you to stay right here and pray for..."

You did not put your will on the Brazen Altar, so you will go into prayer, fighting against what God wants you to do! Then you will get up and speak in tongues all the way to the refrigerator... What! God will say, "Drink it, and you will choke to death, because I told you not to

drink." Before you can become a true intercessor, your will has got to get burned on the Brazen Altar, because when you get inside of the Holy Place, there is only room for ONE WILL. This is why many of us are stuck at "Thy will be done..." Matt. 6:10 We are still warring against the will of God!

**"...for these are antagonistic to each other [continually withstanding and in conflict with each other], so that you are not free but are prevented from doing what you desire to do. But if you are guided (led) by the [Holy] Spirit, you are not subject to the Law. Now the doings (practices) of the flesh are clear (obvious): they are immorality, impurity, indecency, idolatry, sorcery, enmity, strife, jealousy, anger (ill- temper), selfishness, divisions (dissensions), party spirit (factions, sects with peculiar opinions, heresies), envy, drunkenness, carousing, and the like. I warn you beforehand, just as I did previously, that those who do such things shall not inherit the kingdom of God."**
**Galatians 5:17–21, (AMP)**

*Do you see yourself yet?*

I was once invited to preach in Bermuda, and afterwards I decided to stay for a week of vacation. So my mother said, "I am going back to the station, do not get on those mopeds..." She went out to the taxi, and then came back and said, "Nita, especially you." She knows that I am a daredevil. What did I do? I hopped right on a moped after she had said not to do it. I immediately said to myself, "She is full of fear...I am going to ride a moped. I am going to find one on the beach rightnow…"

Of course, I had an accident on the moped, and had to be rushed to the hospital—where I got stitches. When I arrived at the Emergency Room, all the people that were waiting to be helped knew me, because I had been in Bermuda for 7 or 8 days preaching. They were saying things like, "There goes the Prophetess, oh God, they need to help the Prophetess." Everybody that was with me kept saying, "She needs to see a doctor…"

A nurse was sitting there, with her head down, writing. Everybody kept saying, "She needs to see a doctor." I was bleeding profusely. And she said, "What is your name?" I was delirious…crying…and everybody else was upset. The people behind us kept saying, "She needs to see a doctor, she is bleeding!" Unaffected, the nurse said again, "What is your name?" I said, "Juanita." "Last name?" I replied, "Bynum." Then she said, "Oh, you are the evangelist." "Yes." "What is your address?"

I was bleeding, blood was dripping on the floor… but that woman did not care who I was. It was as though she was saying, "Before a doctor can see you, you have got to go through Admitting. I do not care about your gift!"

Church, we have to go through Admitting! Admit it! "I am a liar, a thief…I am jealous, envious, indecent…I do not do things right…I do not have integrity…" God cannot help you until you go through Admitting! And the first question they ask you in Admitting is, "What is your name?" "My name is jealousy, my name is envy, my name is strife, my name is confusion!"

Do not ask for a sedative. Do not even think about taking a painkiller. The Brazen Altar is a death process, not surgery. God is not trying to fix something, or take it out. He is putting you in the fire and burning up that sin! He is getting rid of that "strange fire," and replacing it with the fire of purification!

You say, "I do not understand why I go through so much." You are the one who said that God has called you to be an intercessor! All intercessors, before they can carry the fire, have got to get purified in the fire! Why? You have to know the power of the fire that you carry! You cannot carry the fire to save somebody else's life, asking God to cast the devil out of them—and He has not been able to get the devil out of you!

Are you going through the fire? Good! "Well, I am going through in my marriage." Good! "Pray for my husband…" No, I am praying for you! Stop making intercession for your husband, and pray for yourself! Go back to the Brazen Laver, see what "manner of man" you are, and then get back in the fire! "Oh, Prophetess Bynum, I am going through it on my job…I am praying for my boss." No! God is using your boss to keep you in the fire!

God says, "I am not through with you yet. You are trying to jump off of the fire. Get back on that Brazen Altar… come back here!"

Every time you get comfortable and shout, "Hallelujah," *BAM*…something else hits. Every time you say, "I have the victory!" BAM, something else comes against you, somebody else gets on your nerves, something else goes wrong. Why? God does not want you to think that you have made it! 1 Corinthians 10:12 says,

**"...let anyone who thinks he stands [who feelssure that he has a steadfast mind and is standing firm], take heed lest he fall [into sin]. For no temptation (no trial regarded as enticing to sin, no matter how it comes or where it leads) has overtaken you and laid hold on you that is not common to man [that is, no temptation or trial has come to you that is beyond human resistance and that is notadjusted and adapted and belonging to human experience, and such as man can bear]. But God is faithful [to His Word and to His compassionate nature], and He [can be trusted] not to let you be tempted and tried and assayed beyond your ability and strength of resistance and power to endure, but with the temptation Hewill [always] also provide the way out (the means ofescape to a landing place), that you may be capable and strong and powerful to bear up under it patiently."**
**(AMP)**

Look in the mirror, wash, and then let God put you back in the fire of purification. Grab hold of the horns of the altar, where you will receive salvation, strength, and power! 2 Corinthians 12:7–10 says,

**"And to keep me from being puffed up and too much elated by the exceeding greatness (preeminence) of these revelations, there was given me a thorn (a splinter) in the flesh, a messenger of Satan, to rack and buffet and harass me, to keep me from being excessively exalted. Three times I called upon the Lord and besought [Him] about this and begged that it might depart from me; but He said to me, My grace (My favor and loving-kindness and mercy) is enough for you [sufficient against any danger and enables you to bear the trouble manfully]; for My strength and power are made perfect (fulfilled and completed) and show themselves most effective in [your] weakness. Therefore, I will all the more gladly glory in my weaknesses and infirmities, that the strength and power of Christ (the Messiah) may rest (yes, may pitch a tent over and dwell) upon me! So for the sake of Christ, I am well pleased and take pleasure in infirmities, insults, hardships, persecutions, perplexities and distresses; for when I am weak [in human strength], then am I [truly] strong (able, powerful in divine strength)."**

**(AMP)**

I have to go back to Leviticus 9:24…when that fire came from God, the people fell on their faces. When the real fire from God begins to hit the sanctuaries in this last hour, it will send the people of God to the ground…and it will send them to the altar. Nobody will have to make an altar call.

Not one of us has "made it," no matter who w e are, or how long we have been saved, but God's grace, as symbolized by the number 5 (the width of the altar), and His will, as represented by the number 3 (the godhead, the height of the altar) carry us through to the other side of sacrifice. Stay on the Brazen Altar until God takes you off, so that you can move to the next level in prayer—entering the Holy Place.

## A FINAL WARNING

Let me review. You have repented at the Gate, washed at the Brazen Laver, and offered up your life to God at the Brazen Altar. If you jump off of the altar too soon, you are in danger. The natural sunlight will go down in the Outer Court, and the things you have sacrificed before God will stay on the altar until morning. Lev. 6:9 Your sins and limitations are still being consumed! While the natural light is still shining, you sense that you are in communion with God, because He has allowed the sun to shine. You think that you have been purified, and you can see your way to the Holy Place…

When the sun goes down, the only light you will be able to see is the consuming fire from the Brazen Altar, so you will sit there and "revisit" your past sins. The devil will be saying, "You used to be a prostitute…you used to be this…you are not saved…don't you remember when you used to be that…don't you remember when you did that?"

God commanded the priests to keep the fire burning on the Brazen Altar. If you jump off too soon, the fire could
go out. This is why you have to wait on God's perfect timing to rise from the altar, and head toward the Holy Place.

It is time to move, time to do the work of the Outer Court, and keep moving to the next level in prayer. If you fall down, just come back and do it again. Do whatever is necessary to follow the pattern of the Lord. Keep moving, because the Bible says that when we fall, we have to do the "first works" all over again. [Rev. 2:5] However, Jesus also said that we must work "while it is day: the night cometh, when no man can work." Jn. 9:4

When you are in spiritual darkness, you cannot move. You do not know where you are going. That is why you must move on to the Holy Place, where the Golden Candlestick constantly burns from the fires of your "completed" salvation, and there you will dwell in everlasting light.

# *Selah*

## PAUSE, AND CALMLY THINK OF THAT

**The Brazen Altar The Place of Sacrifice Ex. 27:1–8**

*1. Are you afraid to be purified by the Brazen Altar? Why? Write down anything that you are afraid to give up for God, and then ask Him to help you lay it at His feet. Learn to trust Him, even when it hurts, and to be thankful in every situation.*

*2. Which areas of sin have you not been able to overcome in prayer? Which secret sins are keeping you on the Brazen Altar? Begin the process of confession: first to yourself (out loud, and in your journal), and then to God (in your daily time of prayer). Ask Him for the grace to confess this sin to a "righteous" man or woman, in order to be healed. Then do what He leads you to do. Record the entire process.*

*3. Are people constantly offending you? Is someone telling lies and unjustly defaming you, your family, work, or ministry? Remember what Christ endured on the cross and forgive them—daily, if necessary. Learn how to keep an attitude of forgiveness from a pure heart. Write down their names in your journal, and pray for them every day. Ask for God's will to be done in their lives...then record how God moves on your behalf.*

*4. Are your bills paid? Do you tithe? Do you tell the truth, even about little, insignificant things? Do you have marital problems, or problems handling yourself around the opposite sex? Are there areas of your life that are "out of order" because you have lacked integrity? Take these things to God and ask for His wisdom. Ask Him to lead you in getting help, to turn these areas around for His glory. Journal your progress.*

*5. Do you attend church regularly? Are you "planted" in the spiritual house where God has shown you that you belong? Have you left your home church because the leaders offended you, or left church altogether? Are you offering up "strange fire" before God? Study God's Word, and either make things right, or ask God where your spiritual home is. Then go and submit to their spiritual guidance. Keep journal notes.*

*6. Has God ever called you on a consecration? Have you ever denied your body food, in order to get clearer revelation on what God wants you to do? Study about consecration in the Bible, letting God teach you in this area, and do whatever He leads you to do. Keep detailed notes about your journey.*

*7. Are you learning how to grab the horns of the altar? What does it mean to you now? When everything seems to go wrong, can you still thank God for your salvation? Can you praise Him in the fire? Keep focused on Jesus, and write down everything you are thankful for. Read it every day, if necessary. Add to the list as God prompts you.*

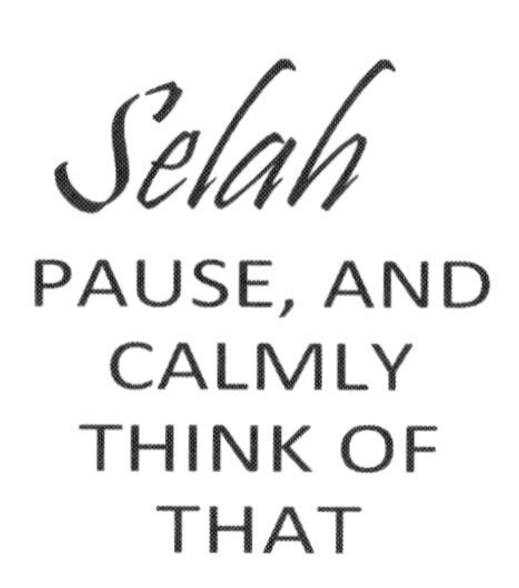


**The Brazen Altar The Place of Sacrifice Ex. 27:1–8**

SELAH

# *Chapter Five*

## THE PRIEST'S CLOTHING: PREPARING TO ENTER THE HOLY PLACE

Moses, whom God had chosen to lead His people out of Egypt, was working with "the flock of Jethro his father in law, the priest of Midian…"
He had led them "from the backside of the desert, and came to the mountain of God." Ex. 3:1
This is significant to our walk of prayer. To me, it marked the spiritual birthing of Moses' Tabernacle in the wilderness...our pattern of prayer from the "finished work"—the physical Tabernacle—which was constructed in the book of Exodus.

Remember what I said about the "completed harvest" at the end of the Preface? To conclude this volume of the series, God is taking us back to our beginnings. Why? Like I said in the beginning, with God everything is already "finished." You are now about to enter into the “harvest” of His finished work in the Outer Court. You have come to the third and final stage in step 3 of God’s pattern of prayer. You have “followed” His pattern to “completed” salvation, and divine preparation to move to the next level…the Holy Place.

Let us continue reading about Moses,

**"And the angel of the Lord appeared unto him in a flame of fire out of the midst of the bush: and he looked, and, behold, the bush burned with fire, and the bush was not consumed. And Moses said, I will now turn aside, and see this great sight, why the bush is not burnt. And when the Lord saw that he turned aside to see, God called unto him out of the midst of the bush, and said, Moses, Moses. And he said, Here am I. And he said, Draw not nigh hither: put off thy shoes from off thy feet, for the place where on thou standest is holy ground. Moreover he said, I am the God of thy father, the God of Abraham, the God of Isaac, and the God of Jacob. And Moses hid his face; for he was afraid to look upon God. And the Lord said, I have surely seen the affliction of my people which are in Egypt, and have heard their cry by reason of their taskmasters; for I know their sorrows; and I am come down to deliver them out of the hand of the Egyptians, and to bring them up out of that land unto a good land and a large, unto a land flowing with milk and honey…Come now therefore; and I will send thee unto Pharaoh, that thou mayest bring forth my people the children of Israel out of Egypt."**

**Exodus 3:2–8 & 10**

First of all, the "burning bush" was not consumed because God was in the midst of it. It was a manifestation of the fire that came down from heaven and lit the Brazen Altar! God is perfect, so the bush was not consumed. So the "bush" in this passage is a "type" of the perfect fire from the third dimension, but also the cleansing fire on the altar of sacrifice—and it symbolizes the "fires" that will burn in the second and third realms of prayer (which I will be covering in volumes II and III). Stay with me. *The best is yet to come.*

Moses had to take off his shoes, his natural means of transportation, before God could speak to him from within the fire, and give him new direction. In prayer, after God gets you off of the Brazen Altar, then and only then, are you able to receive new direction from heaven…and begin to be clothed by the Spirit of God. This is also a warning— though the Brazen Altar is hot—extremely uncomfortable, to the extent that you want to jump off and run, it is a holy place (I will get to this shortly). It is the place of divine "appointment." Having "completed" this level of your salvation at the altar—the final destination of Outer Court Christianity—your life is about to change—forever.

Then something powerful happened, "…Moses hid his face, for he was afraid to look upon God." Proverbs 1:7 says, "The reverent and worshipful fear of the Lord is the beginning and the principal and choice part of knowledge [its starting point and its essence]; but fools despise skillful and godly Wisdom, instruction, and discipline." (AMP) In other words, before you get off of the Brazen Altar (as I said before), you may have knowledge of the Word, but you do not yet have divine revelation…because you must fear God before you can hear from Him, and you must hear from God to serve Him. So God confirmed His pattern to Moses…

**"…I am the God of thy father, the God of Abraham, the God of Isaac, and the God of Jacob."**
**Exodus 3:6, (AMP)**

In other words, He was saying, "I am the God who gave My Word to your fathers. They learned to walk out My revealed Word, and so will you. Their pattern is your pattern. Your life is getting ready to change." This is why we have to experience the first manifestation of "the burning bush" at the Brazen Altar, so that, according to the words of Solomon,

**"That people [you] may know skillful and godly Wisdom and instruction, discern andcomprehend the words of understanding and insight, receive instruction in wise dealing and the discipline of wise thoughtfulness, righteousness, justice, and integrity, that prudence may be given to the simple, and knowledge, discretion, and discernment to the youth—the wise also will hear and increase in learning, and the person of understanding will acquire skill and attain to sound counsel [so that he may be able to steer his course rightly]—that people may understand a proverb and a figure of speech or an enigma with its interpretation, and the words of the wise and their dark sayings or riddles."**

**Proverbs 1:2–6, (AMP)**

You should now have the ability to understand, perceive, discern and comprehend what God will say to you in the Most Holy Place. You will also receive the clothing, and the anointing, to impart His Truth to others, and they will change because God has consecrated you, and completed His Word in you at the Brazen Altar.

So, Moses feared God when he beheld the burning bush, and then God began to share the burdens of His heart. Then He "called"

Moses to deliver His people, Israel. Let me clarify. You will not have the ability to receive the burden of the Lord in prayer until you let God take you off of the Brazen Altar—in His timing. You will not be called to service until after you have been obedient "unto death" Isa. 53:12…until you have "done" the works of Christ (on the Brazen Altar) that He revealed to you at the Brazen Laver.

Having become a "doer" of the Word, you will enter the realm of God's blessings. Do you remember James 1:25 from chapter 3?

**"But he who looks carefully into the faultless law, the [law] of liberty, and is faithful to it and perseveres in looking into it [that means every day in prayer!], being not a heedless listener who forgets [because you think one time, one experience, in God's presence is enough…], but an active doer [who obeys], he shall be blessed in his doing (his life of obedience)."**
**(AMP)**

So you have been cleansed through the Word (in p r a ye r at the Brazen Laver), purified by giving up your will at the Brazen Altar (through sacrificial prayer), and you have come to the place of appointment—the realm that leads you into a life of obedience and service to God—so that others will be set free from the enemy's bondage! That is powerful.

*God is getting ready to put new clothes on you.*

(In case you are thinking that God spoke to Moses before He got to the third realm, you have to remember—God is the third realm! His divine fire (as symbolized in the burning bush) came from the third realm and lit the Brazen Altar. [Lev. 9:24] Moses was standing in the third realm, and that is why he had to take off his sandals! Moses had already gone through the fire! He had already been in the place of service (for his father-in-law, Jethro, a priest) for 40 years in the wilderness! So this wilderness experience, for Moses, was the place of blessing (remember what I said at the beginning of chapter 2?)—because it was the place of His divine appointment, the place that would prepare him to lead Israel through another "wilderness" for the next 40 years!)

*Are you ready to get dressed for the next step of prayer? Are you ready to begin your journey to the Holy Place?*

## THE PRIEST'S CLOTHING

When the priests finished their preparations in the Outer Court, they were required to put on special garments to enter the Holy Place. [Lev. 16:4] First, let me say that God used these garments to prove He never contradicts Himself. Word and Spirit always work in harmony. They always "complement" and "complete" each other, because God works powerfully within the realm of agreement. Jesus said, "Again I tell you, if two of you on earth agree (harmonize together, make a symphony together) about whatever [anything and everything] they may ask, it will come to pass and be done for them by My Father in heaven." Matt. 18:19, (AMP)

Now before you take this scripture and run the wrong direction with it, let me clarify. In verse 18, Jesus told the disciples, "Truly I tell you, whatever you forbid and declare to be improper and unlawful on earth must be what is already forbidden in heaven, and whatever you permit and declare proper and lawful on earth must be what is already permitted in heaven." (AMP) In other words, anything we say and do, as a kingdom of priests, must come from the third realm. You cannot live like the devil and hear God's Word in prayer, and you certainly cannot declare anything in prayer that will come to pass—because you are out of agreement with God!

The priestly garments, and what each piece of clothing represents, the materials, colors, gold, stones, and anointing oil, harmonized with the materials that God instructed Moses to use in the Holy Place.

Are you in harmony with God today? Is your church functioning according to God's pattern? If not, you will never see, or experience, His glory. When you break the pattern, you ignore the works of Christ—and His sacrifice was too costly to ignore. Each piece of your new prayer clothing is custom-made by God, according to His measurements (remember the "outfit" I mentioned at the beginning of chapter 1?). This is the only way He will "commune" with you.

*God is declaring—we must build according to His pattern!*

**"Except the Lord builds the house, they labor in vain who build it; except the Lord keeps the city, the watchman wakes but in vain."**
**Psalm 127:1, (AMP)**

What is God building? What pattern did He create? Mark 11:17 says, "And He [Jesus] taught and said to them, Is it not written, My house shall be called a house of prayer for all the nations? But you have turned it into a den of robbers." (AMP) Watch out! When you neglect the pattern of God, and ignore the works of Christ, you are a thief! You have stolen the sacred things of the Father—to build your own house—and have robbed the people of God's blessings that they are only to receive through Christ.

If you go back to doing your own thing, after you have been through the fire, you are a thief. Your prayers are not just about YOU anymore.

Let us look back briefly at Shadrach, Meshach, and Abednego. The Bible says after they refused to worship the gods of Babylon, "Then these [three] men were bound in their cloaks, their tunics or undergarments, their turbans, and their other clothing, and they were cast into the midst of the burning fiery furnace," Dan. 3:21, (AMP) As I said in chapter 4, God stepped into this fire with them. vs. 24–25 There is a powerful reason for this, but we will go into that later.

When Shadrach, Meshach, and Abednego came out, something even more amazing happened,

**"And the satraps, the deputies, the governors, and the king's counselors gathered around together and saw these men—that the fire had no power upon their bodies, nor was the hair of their head singed; neither were their garments scorched or changed in color or condition, nor had even the smell of smoke clung to them. Then Nebuchadnezzar said, Blessed be the God of Shadrach, Meshach, and Abednego, Who has sent His angel and delivered His servants who believed in, trusted in, and relied on Him! And they set aside the king's command and yielded their bodies rather than serve or worship any god except their own God. Therefore I make a decree that any people, nation, and language that speaks anything amiss against the God of Shadrach, Meshach, and Abednego shall be cut in pieces and their houses be made a dunghill, for there is no other God who can deliver in this way!"**

Shadrach, Meshach, and Abednego honored the sacred things of God, and would not break God's pattern. Therefore, when He "communed" with them in this fire (again, I will break down this revelation in the next volume), God's glory was revealed to the world!

*Do you see the purpose of God?*
*Are you ready to put on your priestly clothing?*

Let us begin by reading about the priestly garments in Leviticus 8:1–3,

**"And the Lord said to Moses, Take Aaron and his sons with him, and the garments, [symbols of their office], and the anointing oil, and the bull of the sin offering, and the two rams, and the basket of unleavened bread; and assemble all the congregation at the door of the Tent of Meeting."**
**(AMP)**

I would like to start by pointing out that God commanded Moses to "take Aaron and his sons." Aaron represents the office of the High Priest, and his sons represent the lower priestly office, which means that God did not tell Moses to choose from among all of the children of Israel. The Lord specifically commanded Moses to get his brother, Aaron, and his sons. To me, this says in order to operate in the "office" of the priesthood, and go into the Tabernacle and behind the veil, we must first be sons ofGod.

We must have a family relationship with God, through the blood of Jesus Christ!

Anyone can come into the Outer Court through salvation, but over-and-above this, we have to honor God, our Father, by being obedient. Ex. 20:12 When it is time to enter the Holy Place, only the obedient children are allowed there. "Many are called…but few are chosen." Matt. 22:14, (AMP) Believers that honor our Father in heaven will move deeper into the heavenly realm. Jesussaid,

**"…whoever does not honor the Son does not honor the Father, who has sent Him. I assure you, most solemnly I tell you, the person whose ears are open to My words [who listens to My message] and believes and trusts in and clings to and relies on Him Who sent Me has (possesses now) eternal life. And he does not come into judgment [does not incur sentence of judgment, will not come under condemnation], but he has already passed over out of death into life."**
**Jn. 5:23–24, (AMP)**

In other words, if you have entered the Gate,

washed at the laver, and sacrificed at the altar according to God's pattern of prayer…you have passed from death into life. You have honored your heavenly Father, and He is going to clothe and prepare you to enter the Holy Place of prayer and intercession.

Let us go back to Leviticus 8:3–8. God told Moses,

**"…and assemble all the congregation at the door of the Tent of Meeting. Moses did as the Lord commanded him, and the congregation was assembled at the door of the Tent of Meeting. Moses told the congregation, This is what the Lord has commanded to be done. Moses brought Aaron and his sons and washed them with water. *[Remember the Brazen Laver?]* He put on Aaron the long undertunic, girded him with the long sash, clothed him with the robe, put the ephod (an upper vestment) upon him, and girded him with the skillfully woven cords attached to the ephod, binding it to him. And Moses put upon Aaron the breastplate; also, he put in the breast plate the Urim and the Thummim [articles upon which the high priest put his hand when seeking the divine will concerning the nation]."**

**(AMP)**

These garments represent everything we do after we enter the Holy Place—whether we will serve in worship and praise, preaching, baptizing, counseling…anything— whatever we will be doing in our service to the Lord must match who Christ is. He is the Gate of 4 colors: white represents His righteousness, blue shows forth His divinity, purple reflects His royalty, and scarlet symbolizes His ultimate sacrifice on the cross.

If our works do not match the works of Christ in the Tabernacle, God will not show up, and the people will lose His blessings. Let me repeat, if the pattern is not "cut" properly, according to God's measurements, then He will not wear it—and if He cannot fit into our clothing, then we are operating in the flesh.

This is why Moses had to wash the priests with water before he clothed them in their priestly garments. Remember, when Christ died on the cross (His altar of sacrifice), they pierced His side, and both blood and water flowed out; so, *His own blood* cleansed Him! Jesus sacrificed and surrendered everything to God, so His righteousness can never be tainted. His righteous garments are bound to Him...*forever*. Let us read Matthew 22:11–14,

**"But when the king came in to view the guest, he looked intently at a man there who had on no wedding garment. And he said, Friend, how did you come in here without putting on the [appropriate] wedding garment? And he was speechless (muzzled, gagged). Then the king said to the attendants, Tie him hand and foot, and throw him into the darkness outside; there will be weeping and grinding of teeth. For many are called (invited and summoned), but few are chosen."**
**(AMP)**

When you are improperly dressed, you cannot even enter the King's presence, much less serve Him. *We are the bride of Christ, a royal priesthood, so we must be dressed accordingly...otherwise, God will allow "common men" to bind our hands and feet.* Many times, we enter into prayer and the enemy is able to bind us (instead of us binding him and his works). We are not able to operate in the things of God, and get things accomplished in the Spirit realm, because we are not properly dressed.

You must be fully dressed in order to enter spiritual service for the Lord. You must have on the proper garments to get through the Door to the Holy Place. Beyond washing…beyond laying down your life…beyond sacrifice—anything that you are going to do—you must be wearing the right spiritual clothing to come before the King. Otherwise, you will be bound in prayer.

When I first started praying at 5:00 a.m., I would get out of bed and go down to the basement (in my living room, or wherever God would send me), and I would walk around and pray in my pajamas. About two months into this process, I got up one morning and the Lord said, "This morning, I want you to get up, get fully dressed, put on some powder, and some lipstick…I want you to dress as if you were going to see a boyfriend." So I started getting up and putting on a decent outfit, like a nice shirt, skirt, and sandals, etc., because He had told me, "I want you to be fully dressed when you come into my presence."

Now I understand.

God requires that we are washed, purified, and properly dressed when we come into His presence in the Holy Place. With this is mind, let us look closely at each piece of the priest's clothing.

## THE TUNIC

The tunic was the first piece of clothing that Moses placed upon Aaron in Leviticus 8:7, "He put on Aaron the long undertunic..." (AMP) This garment matched the wall that surrounded the Outer Court, as well as the first covering over the Tabernacle (we will study this more deeply in the next book). For now, though, let me simply say that both coverings—Aaron's undergarments, and the first layer of the Tabernacle covering, represented righteousness...the foundation of service for God.

If we are going to serve God in intercessory prayer, righteousness must be our foundation.

Added to Aaron's undertunic, Exodus 28:42–43 says,

**"You shall make for them [white] linen trunks to cover their naked flesh, reaching from the waist to the thighs. And they shall be on Aaron and his sons when they go into the Tent of Meeting [the Tabernacle] or when they come near to the altar to minister in the Holy Place, lest they bring iniquity upon themselves and die; it shall be a statute forever to Aaron and to his descendants after him."**
**(AMP)**

Leviticus 16:3–4 brings both pieces, the tunic and trunks, together—

**"But Aaron shall come into the holy enclosure in this way: With a young bull for a sin offering and a ram for a burnt offering. He shall put on the holy linen undergarment, and he shall have the linen breeches upon his body..."**
**(AMP)**

Let me clarify. Though both Aaron and his sons wore the breeches, they wore their tunics in different ways. For the lower priests (his sons), the tunic was their top garment. Aaron wore it underneath his other clothing, tailored specifically for the duties of the High Priest. This confirms there is more than one level when you serve God. Aaron's sons were allowed to serve in the Outer Court, and in the Holy Place; but not in the Most Holy Place. The other Levites performed duties for Aaron and his sons, but they were forbidden to touch the "sacred vessels" of the sanctuary, or the Brazen Altar. Num. 18:23, (AMP)

**"For by the grace (unmerited favor of God) given to me I warn everyone among you not to estimate and think of himself more highly than he ought [not to have an exaggerated opinion of his own importance], but to rate his ability with sober judgment, each according to the degree of faith apportioned by God to him."**

**Romans 12:3, (AMP)**

When God calls you into service, He gives you a level of faith that matches your spiritual assignment. So when He speaks to you from the third realm, and places you in your assigned place, you remain covered by His righteousness as you function at your level of service. Too many of us aspire to be high priests, but we do not have the faith to operate on that level. You have to learn how to be content and productive for God…right where you are.

**"For therein [in the Gospel of Christ] is the righteousness of God revealed from faith to faith: as it is written, the just shall live by faith."**
**Romans 1:17**

In living by faith, you reject your human senses and embrace the righteousness of God. So your spiritual underclothing covers your nakedness—your human nature without God. When you come into the presence of the Lord, these trousers will remind you that God does not need anything "sensual" from you.

God does not need anything from your five senses: what you can see, feel, taste, hear, or touch. Your five senses cannot operate in the spiritual realm of prayer… because they will tell you that a person is still sick. Your "senses" will tell you that a person is still bound. Your five senses will look at the outward circumstances and say, "I have never seen anybody else survive this..." Your "senses" will tell you when a person is in their last stage of AIDS that God cannot heal him.

*Your five senses are the enemies of your faith in a God that answers prayer.*

This is why God puts a covering—a blinding—over your nature with the tunic and breeches. When you are about to enter the realm of the Spirit, your sensualities are no longer needed.

The covering of the private parts also covers the part of our nature that puts confidence in our fleshly abilities as either a man, or a woman. It is not the male or female nature that makes us "strong enough" to enter into effective prayer—we draw our strength from the nature of God. 2 Peter 1:1–8 has a powerful revelation,

**"Simon Peter, a servant and an apostle of Jesus Christ, to them that have obtained like precious faith with us through the righteousness of God and our Savior Jesus Christ: grace and peace be multiplied unto you through the knowledge of God, and of Jesus our Lord, according as his divine power hath given unto us all things that pertain unto life and godliness, through the knowledge of him that hath called us to glory and virtue: whereby are given unto us exceeding great and precious promises:**

**that by these ye might be partakers of the divine nature, having escaped the corruption that is in the world through lust. And beside this, giving all diligence, add to your faith virtue; and to virtue knowledge; and the knowledge temperance; and to temperance patience; and the patience godliness; and to godliness brotherly kindness; and to brotherly kindness charity. For if these things be in you, and abound, they make you that ye *shall* neither be barren nor unfruitful in the knowledge of our Lord Jesus Christ."**

Both your nakedness and old nature are covered as you take on the tunic of Christ's divine nature. Through this, God empowers you to "add to" your faith virtue, knowledge, temperance, patience, godliness, brotherly kindness, and charity. If all these things remain in you, you will be fruitful in prayer (I go into this more in my section on "The Robe"). You will always come out of your prayer closet with the answer. You come out in victory—you will emerge with a word from God. 2 Peter 1:9–10 concludes,

**"But he that lacketh these things is blind, and cannot see afar off, and hath forgotten that he was purged from his old sins", [which means you have forgotten already that you experienced the Brazen Alter and the Brazen Laver. You have been washed from**
**these things]. Wherefore, the rather, brethren, give diligence to make your calling and election sure: for if ye do these things, ye shall never fall..."**

In other words, when you are spiritually blind, you cannot be in the Holy Place, or the Most Holy Place...where the light is supernatural. When you cannot see in the Spirit realm, then you lack the divine nature of God. You are trying to serve a divine God from your lower nature, and it will never happen. There is no match. God will not show up. You need to step back and make your calling and election sure.

You have to be sure that you are called to be an intercessor.

*Here is the most powerful part of the passage…*

**"For so an entrance shall be ministered untoyou abundantly into the everlasting kingdom of our Lord and Saviour Jesus Christ."**
**Vs. 11**

When you are clothed with the white linen tunic and breeches, your old nature is covered by His righteousness. You take on the divine nature of God, which gives you a match in the Spirit, and an entrance into the second and third dimensions of prayer inside of the Tabernacle. So whoever you pray for when you go into these realms of prayer, you will come out having obtained for them the fruit of the kingdom: "…righteousness, and peace, and joy in the Holy Ghost." Rom. 14:17

As sons and daughters of God, Christ has clothed us in His righteousness; we have been washed in His blood. Isaiah 61:10–11 says,

**"I will greatly rejoice in the Lord, my soul willexult in my God; for He has clothed me with the garments of salvation, He has covered me with the robe of righteousness, as a bridegroom decks himself with a garland, and as a bride adorns herself with herjewels.**
**For as [surely as] the earth brings forth its shoots,and as a garden causes what is sown in it to spring forth, so [surely] the Lord God will cause rightness and justice and praise to spring forth before all the nations [through the self-fulfilling power of His word]."**
**(AMP)**

As examples of the self-fulfilling power of God's Word, righteousness—rightness and justice—are supposed to spring forth from our priestly clothing. This means when we come off of the Brazen Altar and put on the clothing of God, we should start doing things differently, "But he who practices truth [who does what is right] comes out into the Light; so that his works may be plainly shown to be what they are—wrought with God [divinely prompted, done with God's help, in dependence upon Him]." Jn. 3:21, (AMP) As we operate in God's rightness and fairness, praise "springs forth," to the glory of God. Revelation 19:7–8 confirms,

**"Let us rejoice and shout for joy [exulting and triumphant]! Let us celebrate and ascribe to Him glory and honor, for the marriage of the Lamb [at last] has come, and His bride has prepared herself."**
**(AMP)**

Finally, we are dressed in fine, radiant linen—dazzling and white for what it signifies— "the righteousness (the upright, just and godly living, deeds, and conduct, and right standing with God) of the saints (God's holy people)." Vs. 8 Jesus said in Matthew 5:14–16,

**"You are the light of the world. A city set on a hill cannot be hidden. Nor do men light a lamp and put it under a peck measure, but on a lampstand, and it gives light to all in the house. Let your light so shine before men that they may see your moral excellence and your praiseworthy, noble, and good deeds and recognize and honor and praise and glorify your Father Who is in heaven."**
**(AMP)**

This is leading us into the Holy Place, because the priests use the fire from the Brazen Altar to light the Golden Candlestick. As you carry that fire from the Outer Court to the Tabernacle, it can be seen in every direction. In the Spirit realm, this means the principalities and powers of darkness can also see it—and they shudder, because they know they cannot follow you into the Holy Place…the enemy knows that his days are numbered.

**"And this is the message [the message of the promise] which we have heard from Him and now are reporting to you: God is Light, and there is no darkness in Him at all [no, not in any way]. [So] if we say we are partakers together and enjoy fellowship with Him when we live and move and are walking about in darkness, we are [both] speaking falsely and do not live and practice the Truth [which the Gospel presents]."** 1 John 1:5–6, (AMP)

As we approach the next level of prayer, our clothing must match the righteousness of Jesus Christ, or we are declaring and living a lie. Remember, Jesus said "I am the way, the truth, and the life" Jn. 14:6…we have come through the Gate, which is "the way," and are approaching the Holy Place, which is symbolic of Truth. If "the truth" is not in us, then we cannot enter the Holy Place, because it does not match the covering of the Tabernacle. "The life," as I said in chapter 1, is the eternal light of God—from heaven—shining in the Most Holy

Place.

The next piece of clothing that Moses placed upon Aaron in Leviticus 8:7 was the girdle, or sash. "He put on Aaron the long undertunic, girded him with the long sash..."

It was told to me that this particular sash (unlike the belt that was described in Exodus 28:8, as part of the Ephod) was attached to the undergarment, so it was never exposed until the Day of Atonement, when Aaron would remove His outer garments to enter the Most Holy Place.

Nevertheless, it always encircled the waist (though nobody could see it).

In prayer, this represents how God works on our behalf. Even though we may not see Him, He has not ceased from His work. He is ever moving on our behalf.

Isaiah 11:4–5 says,

**"But with righteousness and justice shall He judge the poor, and decide with fairness for the meek, the poor and the downtrodden of the earth and He shall smite the earth and the oppressor with the rod of His mouth, and with the breath of His lips He shall slay the wicked. And righteousness shall be the girdle of His waist and faithfulness the girdle of his loins."**
**(AMP)**

A High Priest must always have this attitude—holy, faithful, always on alert to pray or intercede for someone in need. Jesus, our eternal high priest, "…is always living to make petition to God and intercede with Him and intervene" for us. [Heb. 7:25, (AMP)] He never takes off His sash. He is always ready to act in the realm of prayer and intercession.

When you move into intercession, only God knows how long you are going to be there, so your sash (or girdle) strengthens your loins. I remember going to Home Depot for some household fixtures one day, and I noticed that a lot of the workers were wearing those thick, black girdle-belts. So I stopped one guy and asked, 'Why do you have that around your waist? It seems like everybody is wearing them." He responded, "When you are standing on concrete for a long period of time, this band helps to support your legs, so they do not get tired. The band is really holding you from the waist up."

This is when God helped me to realize, when you are standing in intercession, it is like you are standing on concrete. You are standing in a hard place...and since only He knows how long you are going to be in prayer, so you must go into His presence girded. You must also make sure that your breastplate is girded (see the upcomingsection).

Ephesians 6:14 says, "Stand...having your loins girt about with truth..." The power of the sash is two-fold. As Jesus makes intercession for you, your belt of Truth protects you against the lies of the devil. It also strengthens you within, because your loins are a vital part of your body—whatever goes through your loins gets reproduced and multiplied.

Your loins are also the seat of your physical strength, so if you do not put them under the authority of God through wearing your priestly sash, the flesh will try to assume control, "For the flesh lusteth against the Spirit, and the Spirit against the flesh..." Gal. 5:17 Careful, if you do not gird your spirit, the flesh will try to take over.

When you go into intercession for others, it is vital for you to be girded with Truth. Like I said before, you

cannot fight on behalf of another in prayer if Truth is not your sash. When heaven finds no match (in you) on earth, you will be open game for the devil.

## THE ROBE

Going back to Leviticus 8:7, the next piece of clothing was the robe, "He put on Aaron the long undertunic, girded him with the long sash, clothed him with the robe..." (AMP) This robe was blue, which represented position and authority. Attached to it were tassels comprised of seventy- two bells, and seventy-two others that were shaped like pomegranates. The bells represented the "gifts" of the Spirit, and the pomegranates represented the "everlasting fruit" of the Spirit...which means that your "gifts" and "fruit" must match…they must balance out…or God *will not be involved.*

People that always operate in the gifts, without manifesting any fruit, will cause the gifts to constantly clang together. This is not harmony, it is loud-pitched distortion. So if you say that you have been called as an intercessor, and you exercise the "gifts" of the Spirit without exemplifying the fruit, "…love, joy, peace, longsuffering, gentleness, goodness, faith, meekness, temperance…" [Gal. 5:22], something is out of balance (now go back and read 2 Peter 1:1–8).

Let us examine the spiritual "gifts," starting with 1 Corinthians 12:7–10,

**"But the manifestation of the Spirit is given to every man to profit withal. For to one is given by the Spirit the word of wisdom; to another the word of knowledge by the same Spirit; to another faith by the same Spirit; to another the gifts of healing by the same Spirit; to another the working of miracles; to another prophecy; to another discerning of spirits; to another diverse kinds of tongues; to another the interpretation of tongues…"**

**"Having then gifts differing according to the grace that is given to us, whether prophecy, let us prophesy according to the proportion of faith; or ministry, let us wait on our ministering: or he that teacheth, on teaching; or he that exhorteth, on exhortation: he that giveth, let him do it with simplicity; he that ruleth, with diligence; he that sheweth mercy, with cheerfulness."**

**Romans 12:6–8**

**"Wherefore He saith, When He ascended up on high, He led captivity captive, and gave gifts unto men…. And He gave some, apostles; and some, prophets; and some, evangelists; and some, pastors and teachers; for the perfecting of the saints, for the work of the ministry, for the edifying of the body of Christ: Till we all come in the unity of the faith, and of the knowledge of the Son of**

**God, unto a perfect man, unto the measure of the stature of the fullness of Christ: that we henceforth be no more children, tossed to and fro, and carried about with every wind of doctrine, by the sleight of men, and cunning craftiness, whereby they lie in wait to deceive; but speaking the truth in love, may grow up into him in all things, which is the head, even Christ."**

**Ephesians 4:8 & 11–15**

Again, it is not all about YOU anymore. God is strengthening His body, and perfecting His saints. If you are operating in the "gifts" without "fruit," then you are only edifying yourself—and one day, He may tell you, "...Depart from Me..." Matt. 25:41 Even a sorcerer can demonstrate "gifts," but he certainly has no godly "fruit." Let me prove what I am saying by going to Exodus 7:10– 12,

**"And Moses and Aaron went in unto Pharaoh,and they did so as the Lord had commanded: and Aaron cast down his rod before Pharaoh, and before his servants, and it became a serpent. Then Pharaoh also called the wise men and the sorcerers: now the magicians of Egypt, they also did in like manner with their enchantments. For they cast down every man his rod, and they became serpents: but Aaron's rod swallowed up their rods."**

In Bible times, a "rod" was used for "chastising...ruling... throwing...or walking." Strong's 4294, Heb. Watch this. Moses and Aaron exercised their "gift" in obedience to the Lord, "and they did so as the Lord has commanded..." Vs. 10 Aaron's rod "swallowed up" the rods of the magicians. This means when you follow God's pattern, the thing that supports you while you walk—your "fruit"—is the same thing that allows you to exercise your "gifts," and rule over the enemy!

Remember that Aaron received his rod from Moses in Exodus 4 (read the whole chapter). So...God took wood—the limitations of human flesh—and transformed it into a tool of authority. In other words, if you let God anoint what He has put in your hand (like He did for Moses with the stick), you will walk in authority over the enemy in your priestly robe.

Do not operate in your "gifts" without having the "fruit" to match in the Spirit realm.

Operating with "all gifts and no fruit" is a strong deception. This is why most intercessors linger in a danger zone, and often become self-righteous...thinking that nobody is going to heaven but them, and nobody can hear from God but them…because they lack the fruit that would "balance" their gifts. Having snatched the pomegranates off of their garments, they do not reflect the character of God,

**"If I [can] speak in the tongues of men and [even] of angels, but have not love (that reasoning, intentional, spiritual devotion such as is inspired by God's love for and in us), I am only a noisy gong or a clanging cymbal."**
**1 Corinthians 13:1, (AMP)**

When you are entering the realm of true intercession, you are not mean, cocky, or arrogant anymore. You do not act as though, because you have gifts, that you are some

great intercessor, recognized in your church, so everybody else is beneath you. You are not indifferent to others; you do not talk down to people. When God has truly prepared you to enter the Holy Place of prayer, the "everlasting fruitfulness" signified in the pomegranate-shaped tassels has begun to ooze out of you…and the bells have started to make a "joyful" sound—not clanging chatter. Gifts and fruit are in perfect balance.

## THE EPHOD

Now let us move to the next garment listed in Leviticus 8:7, "He put on Aaron the long undertunic, girded him with the long sash, clothed him with the robe, put the ephod (an upper vestment) upon him, and girded him with the skillfully woven cords attached to the ephod, binding it to him." (AMP) According to Exodus 28:8, the ephod had four colors: gold, representing deity; blue, representing divinity; purple, which symbolized the royal One; and scarlet, which symbolized servanthood and humanity. All four had to be "skillfully" woven together.

The ephod clothes you in the garment of the mediator, Jesus Christ. Before it was woven with the other colors, the gold cord had to be beaten out—so when He clothes you with the ephod, you have gone through some trials and tests to get to this level…just like Jesus. Your gold says, "I have already been through the fire; I have survived the worst of it, so I am ready for whatever comes my way in prayer."

Jesus told His disciples in Luke 12:35–37,

**"Keep your loins girded and your lamps burning, [meaning keep the oil of the Spirit, the anointing of God upon you] and be like men who are waiting for their master to return home from the marriage feast, so that when He returns from the wedding and comes and knocks, they may open to Him immediately.**
**Blessed (happy, fortunate, and to be envied) are those servants whom the master finds awake and alert and watching when he comes. Truly I say to you, he will gird himself and have them recline at table and will come and serve them!"**
**(AMP)**

When the Spirit of the Lord finds us girded, He responds by girding Himself to us—so that we can relax at His table. This means we have a part to play in the process of prayer; first, we must surrender to God, and then we have to walk in prayer until the Spirit of the Lord comes and takes over. When that happens, we can ungird ourselves. He girds Himself and begins to serve us; answering our prayers, and ministering to us about what we brought to Him.

When God sees that we are willing to take on His burden, He will give us rest from our labor and begin to do the work on our behalf.

Christ becomes the mediator, our ultimate intercessor.

This takes me back to John 13:1–5,

**"[Now] before the Passover feast began, Jesus knew (was fully aware) that the time had come for Him to leave this world and return to the Father. And as He had loved those who were His own in the world, He loved them to the last and to the highest degree.**
**So [it was] during supper, Satan having already put the thought of betraying Jesus in the heart of Judas Iscariot, Simon's son, [That] Jesus knowing (fully aware) that the Father had put everything into His hands, and that He had come from God and was [now] returning to God, got up from supper, took off His garments, and taking a [servant's] towel, He fastened it around His waist. Then He poured water into the washbasin and began to wash the disciples' feet and to wipe them with the [servant's] towel with which He was girded."**
**(AMP)**

If Jesus girded Himself before operating in the Spirit, then we should definitely follow His example. Why? We have no legal right to break the pattern of God! If you break His pattern, you will expose yourself to danger, and you will not be "girded" to serve the spiritual needs of others. Listen to me, saint,

You must allow God to "gird" you in prayer. Otherwise, you are on your own.

As a kingdom of priests, we have been commanded to enter into His rest. Heb. 3:7–11 Having done this, we can serve others as He has served us, which is the manifestation of Christ's humility. This is the essence of servanthood, willingly taking up the burden of the Lord—taking on somebody else's situation, somebody else's circumstances—and becoming a servant to them in prayer. Let us look at Philippians 2:4–8,

**"Let each of you esteem and look upon and be concerned for not [merely] his own interests, but also each for the interests of others. Let this same attitude and purpose and [humble] mind be in you which was in Christ Jesus: [Let Him be your example in humility:] Who, although being essentially one with God and in the form of God [possessing the fullness of the attributes which make God God], did not think this equality with God was a thing to be eagerly grasped or retained, but stripped Himself [of all privileges and rightful dignity], so as to assume the guise of a**

**servant (slave), in that He became like men and was born a human being. And after He had appeared in human form, He abased and humbled Himself [still further] and carried His obedience to the extreme of death, even the death of the cross!"**
**(AMP)**

You cannot walk in humility, unless you have been "girded" by Christ.

His ephod will help you to serve others, especially those who are weak or of a lesser status—with the grace that He gives—to help the immature in Christ come to maturity. I have heard intercessors say, "God showed me this about so-and-so…" and then they turn around and say, "I do not have patience for that." If this is you, do you really think that you are functioning in a way that is pleasing to God? Are you truly girded with the ephod of the Lord? I do not think so.

Here is a powerful example. Two onyx stones were on the shoulders of the ephod, and twelve stones were on the breastplate. Both were inscribed with the twelve tribes of Israel, but in a different order. On the shoulder of the ephod, they were in the order of their birthright. On the breastplate, they were in a different order, according to the will of God. What does this mean?

You may know something, and carry the burden of this person on your shoulders—how she was born in the Spirit, how she is doing in the natural right now, and her family background (i.e., all of her uncles were alcoholics, and that is why she is an alcoholic). You have to turn around, bind this prayer request to your heart (breastplate), and seek God to reveal His will. When you come out with a word from the Lord, God illuminates and perfects what you brought before Him (I will explain this more in the next section).

You look on your shoulder and see what she used to be, and then look at the breastplate, and give glory
to God for what He has done.

This is how we can be confident that God is able to do "…exceedingly, abundantly above all that we could ask or think," not according to the power that is on our shoulder, but His power that works within us. 2 Corinthians 4:18 says, "…we look not on the things which are seen, but at the things which are not seen: for the things which are seen are temporal; but the things which are not seen are eternal."

## THE BREASTPLATE

Let us continue by going back to Leviticus 8:8, "And Moses put upon Aaron the breastplate; also he put in the breastplate the Urim and the Thummim [articles upon which the high priest put his hand when seeking the divine will concerning the nation]." (AMP) This garment is vital to becoming an intercessor. In the pocket of the breastplate was a pouch containing the Urim and the Thummim, and a parchment that had the divine name of God written on it. *Urim* means "light" and *Thummim* means "completeness." God communicated with the High Priest when these elements caused individual letters oftribal names to light up. The Urim would light the letters, and the Thummim represented that if the letters were read in the proper order, a complete and true answer had been received for the nation's request to God. God's "Ineffable Name" in the breastplate would activate the Urim and the Thummim, and bring His divine direction to earth.

This is why Jesus said to His disciples, "… whatsoever ye shall ask in my name, that I will do, that the Father may be glorified in the Son." Jn. 14:13 When you have made it through the fire, all the way to the Holy Place… and you call upon the name of Jesus saying, "Father, I thank You and ask that You would do this…" or "fix this situation" in His divine name, it ignites your prayers and "activates" the answer from God.

The breastplate also represents the people you carry to God in prayer. I compare the breastplate to a prayer request list…names that you have written down to take with you when you enter the Holy Place. These people remain "bound" to your chest, so they stay close to your heart. This is when you know God has truly "girded" you, and given you His intercessory burdens.

When you are girded with the breastplate, and call on Jesus' name in prayer; not only will light come into the situation, God will perfect the things that you have carried to Him.

## THE MITER

The next piece of clothing listed in Leviticus 8:9 is the miter, or turban, "And he put the turban or miter on his head; on it, in front, Moses put the shining gold plate, the holy diadem, as the Lord commanded him." (AMP)

The miter was like a hat, with one distinguishing feature…the holy crown. This crown was actually a golden plate that was mounted on the front of the miter. It had an inscription that read, "Holy unto The Lord," which represented atonement and enabled Israel to offer "acceptable" sacrifices to God on the Brazen Altar. It symbolized that the nation of Israel was completely devoted to God and His service, and reminded the priests never to take holiness for granted as they carried out their duties.

The miter can be likened to the "helmet of salvation" in Ephesians 6:17. According to the rabbinical teachings, the crown denoted that, at all times, the priest was to conduct his life worthy of the name he wore. Let us look at Ephesians 4:1–3,

**"I therefore, the prisoner for the Lord, appeal to *and* beg you to walk (lead a life) worthy of the [divine] calling to which you have been called [with behavior that is a credit to the summons to God's service, living as becomes you] with complete lowliness of mind (humility) and meekness (unselfishness, gentleness, mildness), with patience, bearing with one another *and* making allowances because you love one another. Be eager and strive earnestly to guard and keep the harmony *and* oneness of [and produced by] the Spirit in the binding power of peace."**
**(AMP)**

## YOU ARE A LIVING TABERNACLE

So here you are…a royal priest before God. He has summoned you to serve others in prayer, and has clothed you with the garments of preparation to enter the Holy Place. As you carry the light from the Brazen Altar to the door of the Tabernacle, your deeds must match the flame that you carry. You have become the light of the world, and you are entering the realm where you will bear the burden of the

Lord in prayer…keeping in harmony with Him, and working in harmony with others.

A Hebrew commentary states, "The clothes of Aaron and his sons invested them with the visible emblems of their holiness and marked them as distinct functions, separating them from the rest of the nation…when the priests were clothed in their garments, the priesthood was upon them, and when they were not clothed in the

priestly garments, the priesthood was not upon them." Ex.29:5

The colors and characteristics of the Tabernacle were reflected in the priestly garments, creating a match in the Spirit realm…forever associating the priesthood with the Tabernacle. This clothing was given to them "for glory and splendor." Ex. 28:2, Chumash Glory, because of their God- given abilities, and splendor because of their own efforts to serve God. What does this mean? After God takes you off of the Brazen Altar—a combination of wood and bronze that stands 3 cubits high and

5 cubits wide—you are a product of the finished work of the godhead through grace, that has enabled you to become a "doer" of the Word.

Now, everyone will see the "new you," *even the enemy.* He will know that His time is short (as it concerns your assignment), because you are moving into the realm of intercession…you have been washed at the Brazen Laver, purified at the altar, and you are going to the next level.

**"…For we are the temple of the living God; even as God said, I will dwell in and with and among them and will walk in and with and among them, and I will be their God, and they shall be My people."**
**2 Corinthians 6:16, (AMP)**

If your life does not exemplify the characteristics of your priestly clothing, then the priesthood—and the anointing to be an intercessor—is not upon you. If there is no

harmony between the "colors" in your life and those in the Tabernacle, you will not experience the proper flow of the Spirit in prayer.

Make "your calling and election sure" today, because you are the temple of the Holy

Ghost, a living, breathing Tabernacle—which makes it possible for you to enter His divine presence. You can approach God right now, you do not have to wait until you get to heaven—*go to Him in your spirit man.* This is the final match, spirit to Spirit, through His pattern ofprayer,

**"A time will come…indeed it is already here, when the true (genuine) worshippers will worship the Father in spirit and in truth (reality); for the Father is seeking just such people as these as His worshipers.**
**God is a Spirit (a spiritual Being) and those who worship Him must worship *Him* in spirit and in truth (reality)."**
**John 4:23–24, (AMP)**

As you move closer to the Holy Place, holding the fire from your sacrifice on the Brazen Altar…you will suddenly realize what is real, and what is not. Your old prayer life is gone. Suddenly…all things have "become new." 2 Cor. 5:17 Your clothes will have changed, and you will see the same colors you are wearing straight ahead of you—*on the Door to the Holy Place*—a perfect match…and you will know that when you get there, God is going to meet with you.

You have been born "…for *such* a time as this..." Esther 4:14

Like Moses, you will never be the same.

Like Moses, you have discovered the pattern of God in prayer. You persevered and "followed" the Lord through every step of His pattern. Like Moses, you have been divinely summoned by God to change the course of this world.

**Are you ready to go to the next level of prayer?**

***Are you ready to enter the Holy Place?***

Stay with me…*the best is yet to come.*

**The Priest's Clothing**
**Preparing to Enter The Holy Place Lev. 8:7–9**

*1. Have you ever had a "burning bush" experience with God? Are you beginning to discern His presence more accurately now that He has taken you off of the Brazen Altar? What is being birthed in your spirit as He dresses you to enter the Holy Place of intercession? Write it down.*

*2. Are you beginning to receive insight and understanding of God's Word on a deeper level? Look back through your Bible study notes, and journal, and record these new revelations. Begin to ask God what He wants you to do as you prepare to serve Him in the Holy Place. Write down His reply.*

*3. Examine your life. Can you look in the mirror of God's Word and see your new tunic of righteousness? Have you become a "doer" of the Word, consistently? Write down the areas where God has given you the greatest testimonies.*

*4. Are your loins "girded" with your priestly*

*sash? Are you using it faithfully, whenever you need the strength of the Lord? Record these experiences in your journal.*

*5. Are you beginning to experience new power in prayer? Is your robe of divine authority equally balanced with the fruit of righteousness, and your spiritual gifts? Write a list of your godly character traits, alongside of your spiritual gifts. Is there a balance? If not, address areas that are lacking through prayer—and then wash, sacrifice, and start the list again.*

*6. Do you keep the 4 works of Christ girded to your ephod? Have you endured in prayer to the point that Christ will come and take over, leading you in intercession? Are you walking in humility, toward God and man? Journal your progress.*

*7. Is your breastplate securely fastened? Who is God putting on your heart to carry into the place of prayer? Write their names on your prayer list and begin to ask God to lead you in prayer on their behalf. Be available if they need you, always lead them to God, and do everything in Jesus' name.*

*8. Is your turban securely in place, confirming to everyone that you are "Holy unto the Lord"? Are you walking, steadily and gracefully, toward the Holy Place? Is a passion for prayer stirring within you? Ask God to lead you into intercession, and start a new journal for a new day. You are about to enter the next level of prayer.*

## The Priest's Clothing
## Preparing to Enter The Holy Place Lev.8:7–9

SELAH

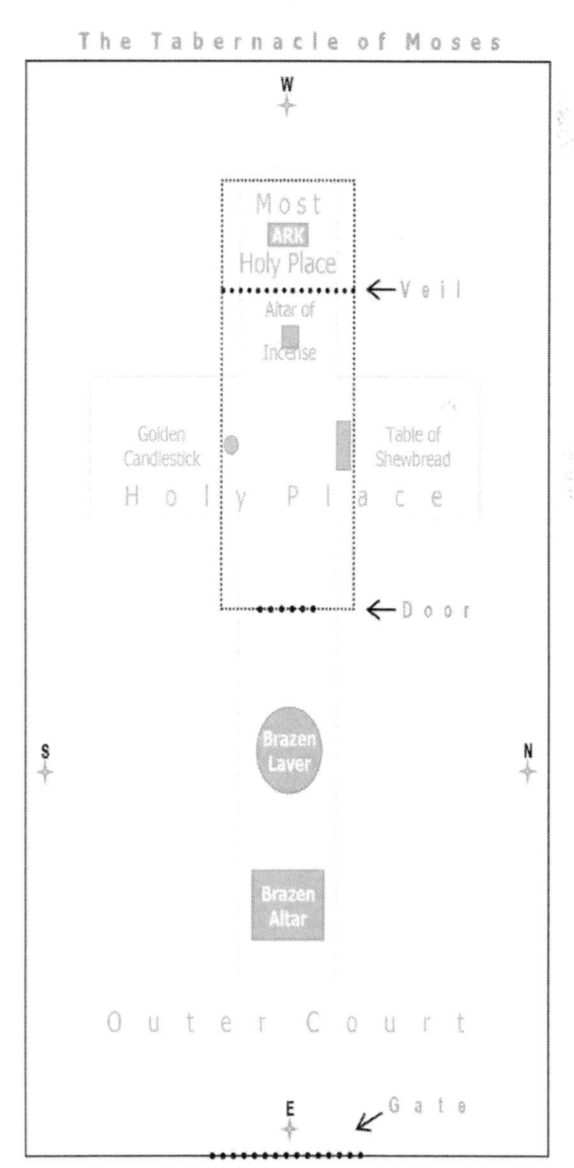

The Cross in the Tabernacle Furniture

Made in the USA
Columbia, SC
30 December 2017